History of Germany

Leon Amiel Publisher
New York

Concise History of Great Nations
General Editor: Otto Zierer

Otto Zierer Germany

Contents

Translation by G. Irvins

Illustration on jacket: Wilhelm I being proclaimed Emperor of Germany, at Versailles, on January 18 1871.
Title page: Coronation of the last Emperor, Francis II, on July 14 1972, in Frankfurt cathedral.

Credits:
Bavaria 13, 89, 100, 104, 105, 116, 120, 121. Bernisches Historisches Museum 8. Biblioteca Ambrosiana 29. Bildarchiv Preußischer Kulturbesitz jacket 9, 10, 11, 13, 17, 48, 49, 50, 52, 65, 71, 73, 77, 80, 81, 84, 88, 93, 95, 101, 105, 108, 109, 113, 117, 120. Bullot 76, 92. Burgerbibliothek, Bern 24. Caisse National des Monuments Historiques 16. Germanisches Nationalmuseum 44. Giraudon 76, 81, 96, 98. Habermann 72. Hamburger Kunsthalle 85. Holle 4/5. Krupp 97. Lossen Foto 32. Media 112. Österr. National-Bibliothek 46, 47. Orlandini 12. Rheinisches Landesmuseum 20. Roger-Violett 26, 46, 56. Scala 28. Soldatino 8, 36, 69. Staatsarchiv Wien 40. Werbefotograf 45.

Published 1977 by Leon Amiel Publisher
31 West 46th Street,
New York, N.Y. 10036,
U.S.A.

Library of Congress Catalog Card No. 77-73091
I.S.B.N. No. 0-8148-0673-2

© Media Books S. A., Nyon, 1976
Printed in Germany by Mohndruck Reinhard Mohn OHG, Gütersloh

1 From the Carolingians to the Rise of the German Empire

When the Carolingians (751–911) began to rule over the Kingdom of the Franks, the world to the north of the defunct Roman Empire, hitherto disrupted by tribal wanderings (Völkerwanderung) and Hunnish battles, had calmed down to some extent. The races and tribes which were to determine the history of the Middle Ages had taken their places on the stage.

The Franks, a Germanic tribe who had crossed the Lower and Middle Rhine, had asserted their claim to one single state on land which had formerly been a Roman province (Gaul).

There were three reasons for this: firstly, in 496 they had espoused the Catholic form of Christianity, and were therefore not in opposition to the subjugated native population. Secondly, they took the land as farmers and held with their plows what they had won with their swords. And thirdly, on both sides of the Rhine they maintained a living attachment to their Germanic fatherland. This land of their origin was—as the chroniclers report—four-fifths forest, with scarcely any pathways. Only in a few regions, along the Rhine and Danube, where the Romans had once been, were there any towns, roads and superior civilisation. Germania itself, the nucleus of the future Germany, was the rural territory of Franks, Saxons, Thuringians, Hessians, Swabians (Alamans) and Bavarians, and was only loosely connected to the Carolingian empire.

In about the seventh century, missionaries came to these still wild regions from the monasteries of Ireland, Scotland, and later, England: missionaries such as Fridolin, Kolumban, Gallus and Kilian.

However, this early mission only affected those regions which had once lain behind the Roman frontier and the *limes*, and which had for centuries been accustomed to look politically and culturally to Rome: especially Alamania and Bavaria. All large-scale missionary and civilisation work, the creation of order in regions won over to the new doctrine, and the conversion of further Germanic provinces to Christianity, were all reserved for the Anglo-Saxon mission, especially for its leading representative, Boniface. He became the apostle of the Germans and the founder of the German Church Province (about 720–55).

Supported by the political power of the Frankish kings, Boniface, along with the Anglo-Saxon Willibrord, first of all preached the Gospel to the Frisians; he later went to central and southern Germany and was ordained a bishop in Rome. Then he travelled to Thuringia and Hesse, where he founded the famous abbey at Fulda. He brought religious order to Bavaria, founded Würzburg and Paderborn monastery and summoned the first Church conventions. Boniface was finally made Archbishop at Mainz—which was to become the center of the Church in Germany—within the crumbled walls of the former seat of Roman power. Later archbishoprics were founded at Trier and Cologne, which had once been Roman imperial seats.

At a time when Ostrogoths and Romans were fighting over Italy, the monastic order of the Benedictines was brought into being by Benedict of Nursia (529) on Monte Cassino. Their motto was: *ora et labora,* "pray and work." The learned Cassiodorus Senator, Theodoric's former chancellor, who was later a Benedictine, added: "... and copy books, so that the knowledge and culture of the Ancient World may be saved and carried over to the new times."

In the 7th and 8th centuries, monasteries of this order arose at the most favorable places on German soil and became missions and cultural centers. The pious monks set up schools for the Alamanic, Bavarian, Hessian, Thuringian or Saxon children of peasants and nobles: they ght improved methods of stockbreeding and fruit tree cultivation; they brought improved seedcorn, established workshops for almost-forgotten handicrafts; they taught the art of brewing beer, building with brick and stone, they painted, drew, wrote books and taught the seven noble school arts (scholasticism).

It was the monasteries and the sense of order introduced by the great missionary Boniface which led the German tribes out of a time of general brutality, barbarism and dissoluteness to superior morality, the beginnings of social thinking and ecclesiastical penitence. The great ancient culture had been broken down by the *Völkerwanderung* and by the emergence of relatively barbaric races of peasants and warriors; moral and civic order was now no longer a matter of brute force.

Thus there existed among the more educated members of society, but also among the common people, a desire for some higher aim in life, and a strong feeling of opposition to the lust for power of the land-robbers and the unchecked passions of the rulers. The Church took advantage of this yearning in order to build up, by arduous toil, her new western spiritual empire. Boniface bound the German Church Order to Rome and thereby paved the way for a development which further determined the Middle Ages.

This idea of uniting the political power obtained at the end of the *Völkerwanderung* with the stabilizing

spiritual strength of the Church, thereby regaining control of the moribund empire, now became quite widespread in Europe as a whole.

It was the Frankish kingdom of the Merovingians which emerged as the strongest power from the ruins left by centuries of chaos. However, the Merovingians slaughtered each other in internal battles, weakened the Frankish kingdom ever further by divisions, fratricidal wars and the degeneration of the ruling house. Behind these, an efficient stock of ordinary military men—the "Karals" or stewards—had developed and taken over the ruling power in their position of *majordomus*, or majordomo. One of these, Charles Martell, welded together a great number of the German tribes, and in 732, near Poitiers, with the strength of the free militia, he routed an army of Arabs, Muslims and Moors who were advancing from Spain.

With keen political insight, the Roman Pope recognised in Charles Mar-

tell the future leader of the western world, and offered him alliance and cooperation. Charles did not yet realise the possibilities of such a union; however, his son, Pepin (751–768) understood. He directed the Frankish might against the Lombards in Italy, who were oppressing the Pope; he permitted the founding of the Church State and played the role of the Church's strong arm.

Thanks were not wanting: Pope Zachary agreed to the promotion of Pepin to Frankish King, and in 754 Pope Stephen II anointed the new King of the Franks at St. Denis. One of history's lucky breaks brought Charlemagne to power. According to Frankish peasant custom, the realm was divided up among the sons when a ruler died. Now it happened that, three generations after Charles Martell, only one heir remained, and the kingdom, with all its bordering duchies in Frisia, Alamania, Bavaria, Thuringia and Hesse, passed as a whole into the hands of a significant man.

And Charlemagne fulfilled what his religious partner hoped of him: he created the nucleus of a new Empire in the West, whose vanguard consisted of missionaries and monks, those black-robed purveyors of the cultural heritage of Europe.

In repeated and protracted wars, Charlemagne and the Frankish militia subdued the Saxons, that gigantic, defiant tribe which was most bitterly opposed to the Christian religion, and, consequently to the concept of the Empire. Once again it was those of the Teutons who, in Roman times, had already done their best to resist the Mediterranean spirit and empire, who now burned down the monasteries on the Weser and the Eider, and who looked to the north instead of to Rome. However, the supremacy of a well-organised and better-armed Frankish king finally defeated Duke Witikind. On the Aller thousands of Saxons were slain, and at the mouth of the Elbe the Frankish fortress of Hamburg was established; even the Holstens and the Jutes had to bow down to the Franks. Thus Charlemagne extended the limits of the Empire as far as the Elbe, Eider and Saale.

The ever-eccentric Bavarians were robbed of their tribal duchy, Duke Tassilo was sent to a monastery, and the land was ruled by Charlemagne's people. Even in this area the Empire, and with it, Christianity, were spreading eastwards: in 796 Charlemagne founded the Archbishopric of Salzburg and annexed the eastern Bavarian March-lands to his empire. In Italy the Franks brought the Lombards under their rule, while, in the northern reaches of his empire, Charlemagne defeated the Frisians and Danes, thereby driving these freedom-loving peasants onto ships,

from which they raided coasts and estuaries as Norman or Viking pirates.

A great empire was in the making; Charlemagne defined its limits by means of campaigns against the Slavs, Avars and Arabs. Between Aachen (Aix-la-Chapelle), his favorite seat of power, and Ravenna, Rome determined the course of history.

A renaissance of Roman order seemed to be preparing itself. Charlemagne had roads built, enacted laws and decrees which governed all aspects of life; he divided the empire into districts and margravedoms, administered dukedoms, held parliaments and, in keeping with an old Germanic custom, assembled the free peasant-warriors on the Field of May, for a military parade and court day.

As Protector of the Church, Charlemagne built monasteries, schools and model farms, where his "stewards" governed to set an example and instruct the neighboring peasants *(Huber)*.

At the court at Aachen, on ancient Roman soil, his academics gathered together: they were the Anglo-Saxon Alkuin, a great teacher, Paulus Diakonus, the historian, and the master builder Einhard, who built Charlemagne's cathedral and palace, copying models at Ravenna. From this academy the first move towards a collection of German heroic songs was made; the lost arts began to come alive again.

In order to govern this great empire, which today seems an impossible

task in view of the condition of transport and communications at the time, Charlemagne sent out envoys to the districts, and himself moved about from one of his "Imperial Courts," which were called Palatinates *(Pfalz)*, after Caesar's former seat of power at Palatium, to another: he was incessantly active as founder, controller and law-maker. It was no wonder that Pope Leo II, to whose aid he again rushed with military support against Italian enemies, crowned him Roman Emperor on New Year's Eve in the year 800.

This too was a sign of history, that the crown of the Caesars should be bestowed on the Franks by the Church and the Pope. This established *dependence*.

Under Pepin and Charlemagne,

however, a process began in the Frankish and German lands, which was to develop to the disadvantage of the nation. A complete feudal system came into being, and created a supremacy of power for the great landowners, the nobles and the ever land-hungry Church.

The free possession of a farm was bound up with duties. All free peasant-warriors had the duty to stand armed for the militia. As campaigns and wars were numerous, the farms and the farmers' fortune suffered greatly. Therefore many of them chose voluntary dependence, or "vassalage" under lords of the manor or monasteries, who then relieved them of some of the burdensome army duties in return for certain duties and feudal dues. The status of the free

Charlemagne symbolically offers the Virgin a model of the cathedral of Aix-la-Chapelle, which he had founded. Detail from Charlemagne's Reliquary.

farmer began to disappear. All too many of them had their long hair (symbol of freedom) cut off and became serfs *(Gescherte)*.

Under these conditions, only a very strong personality could hold together an empire of opposing tribes and peoples. Charlemagne's successor, his son Ludwig (Louis) the Pious (814–840) was not such a man.

He was originally intended for the priesthood, but came to the throne because of the premature deaths of his more forceful brothers Pepin and Charles. The reins of government were soon drawn from the hands of this learned man, who inspired many pious poems, such as the "Heliand," and spent his time reading the richly-decorated books of the Gospel. Under him the monastery of Corwey on the Weser was founded, Gandersheim blossomed forth, in Mainz Alkium's favorite scholar, Hrabanus Maurus—the *Praeceptor Germaniae*—was teaching; the monastery schools were teaching the *trivium* of grammar, rhetoric and logic, and the *quadrivium* of arithmetics, geometry, music and astronomy. In Reichenau, where Walafried Strabo was teaching, in St. Gallen with Notker and Ekkehard, or in the Bavarian monasteries of Benediktbeuren, Tegernsee, Wessobrunn, Niederaltaich or St. Emmeran, famous monastery schools emerged; at the seats of bishops and archbishops, such as Metz, Constance, Augsburg, Freising, Salzburg, Regensburg, Eichstätt, Passau or Würzburg, the forerunners of the universities, the cathedral schools, were growing. However, what use was all this activity when the political affairs of the Empire were heading for disaster?

After only a few years Ludwig the Pious made his eldest son co-emperor and gave parts of the realm in the east and west to his other sons, Pepin and Ludwig. Then, after the death of his first wife, he married the scheming "Black Judith" from the Alamanic race of the Welfs, and had another son, Charles. When he gave in to Judith's wishes and made over parts of the Empire to this late-born son, at the expense of his elder sons, it led to protracted civil wars.

On the Lügenfelde, near Colmar, deserted by his vassals, the betrayed Emperor was forced by his sons to publicly acknowledge his sins, his weapons were taken from him, his sword removed, and he was dressed in serf's clothing (833).

The struggle for Carolingia was underway. Normans plundered and ravaged across the Frankish rivers and attacked the coasts. In the south the Saracens were oppressing southern Italy and Sicily; Avars and Huns began to stir in the east. A league of farmers, calling themselves the *"Frilinge"* or *"Stellinga"* rose up against the big land-owners.

When the armies of Charles, that is the West Franks, and of Ludwig, who called himself "the German," united near Strasburg, their pact was written and sworn in two languages: the army coming from France used the *Romance* language—a language based on Latin which had evolved among the people who had settled in Gaul—, the others used *Tiudisker,* or the Frankish dialect, which later developed into the German language; all this was in 842. The partition of the empire was laid down in the Treaty of Verdun (843): Lothar received, besides the Imperial Dignity, the central part of the empire, later named after him as Lotharingen (Lorraine)—from the mouths of the Schelde and Rhine, across Lorraine, Alsace, Burgundy and as far as Italy; Charles was to rule France, and Ludwig the eastern regions now known as Germany.

Charlemagne conferring the kingdom of Italy on his youngest son Pippin.
After the deaths of Pippin in 810 and his elder brother in 811, the
imperial inheritance went undivided to the younger son, Louis the Pious.
This copy of a 9th-century drawing was made in the 10th century.

The century ended in chaotic defensive battles against Normans, Saracens, Avars and Slavs; the race of the Carolingians was sinking into anarchy.

When, in 896, the German princes unceremoniously elected as king Arnulf von Kärnten, one of the last of the Carolingians, this meant a break in the transmission of the Eastern Empire, which, until then, had recognised the law of succession. They were returning to the old Germanic folk-custom of election. Yet not even Arnulf was able to save either the Empire or the young German state. The atmosphere of the times is reflected in the *Weltuntergangslied* (song of doom) of the last days of the Carolingians: the time of the hatchet and the wolf.

The Normans burned down Cambrai, Maastricht, Liège, Cologne, the monasteries of Prüm, Stablo and Malmedy, the castles at Jülich, Zülpich and Neuss, made the Palatinate Chapel at Aachen into a stable, until the united forces of the Germans finally succeeded in driving them back. After Arnulf's death the German land lapsed more and more into chaos. Officials who had earlier administered Carolingia, began to set themselves up as independent princes; in the east, Hungarian horsemen—remnants of the Hunnish *Völkerwanderung*—began to threaten the borderlands. The rulers of the German districts were at war with each other, each trying to increase his own lands. In 911 the Germans in the Palatinate at Forchheim elected Conrad of Franconia the new king.

This new king-elect spent his short reign (until 918) in senseless struggles against the Saxon duke, in feeble counter-attacks on the Hungarians, who had by this time hade succeeded in advancing as far as Lake Constance

and the Rhine, and in disputes about his Franconian inheritance.

When he died, he left the crown to his most powerful opponent, Henry of Saxony, the only man with enough power and talent to save the German kingdom. At first, Henry I (918–936) was recognized as king only by the Saxons and the Franks around the river Main, but he at once subdued the Bavarians and the Swabians (Alamans), and later even forced Duke Giselbert of Lorraine, who had annexed his land to France, to acknowledge him.

Firstly, Henry negotiated a nine-year truce for the Saxons and the Thuringians with the Hungarians. He used this time to build walled military settlements, protected by palisades; these he constructed at strategic places. He became the founder of towns and gathered civilians, or *"burghers"* behind the fortifications. Meanwhile the old Roman towns along the Rhine, Main and Danube had revived, and began to live again: laborers, nobles with their solid townhouses, traders, and clerics, but also landowners, all settled here for security and to establish markets. In Saxony and Thuringia, the new towns being built, were to face the full force of a Hungarian attack, and halt the advance of the Slavs.

King Henry also created a new cavalry. In most cases the gift of property was sufficient remuneration for knightly services. Travelling warriors were held dependent on the manors: a new status was developing—that of the knight. With this cavalry, supported by the new fortified strongholds, King Henry annihilated the Hungarians in 933 at the Unstrutt. He was left with the task of fixing more firmly the German kingdom in its tribal dukedoms. By bestowing the

Below, left: Lothaire, elder son of Louis the Pious, received the imperial crown in 817, through the "ordinatio imperii". When his brothers rebelled against him he had to agree to share out the Empire (Treaty of Verdun, 843).

Freigrafschaft on Duke Rudolf of Burgundy, he obtained the "Holy Lance", the relic with which Longinus had pierced Christ's side. He had a black cloth attached to this priceless holy relic, with St. Michael embroidered in gold. This banner was thenceforth to serve as standard to a united German militia. Black and gold became the imperial colors of the dynasty, and "German Michael" became the symbol of a nation growing together. This national feeling was a fragile shoot, while the various tribal feelings grew in strength. The glossaries of Kassel praise the intellectual superiority of the Bavarians; by advancing against the Celtic "Welsh" people of the Alps, the Swabian tribe asserted itself; the Franks expressed their individuality through Otfried's writing; in Saxony they glorified Witikind's Saxon history; only the Franks along the Rhine and in Lorraine, as half-castes, enjoyed little trust.

In this time of the political beginnings of the German kingdom, the original strength of Germania at the same time brought forth a new style of art and building, which was later, because of its origins, known as *Romanesque*.

However, Germany did not yet ex-

scious solidarity of the Germans, that after Henry I's death, his son Otto I (936–973), who was only twenty-four years old, was elected King by the princes at Aachen, and crowned in Mainz by the archbishop.

At the beginning he too had to fight against tribal dukes in Franconia, Lorraine, and even in his own land of Saxony, but he emerged victorious from these troubles. The king now sent his representatives, *Pfalzgrafen* (counts), to each of the dukedoms.

Otto set the powers of the Church against the weight of the dukes, by providing the archbishops, bishops and abbots with rich estates; he accorded them regal rights (regalia), and reserved for himself the power of enfeoffment and endowment of this clerical class, who were celibate, and therefore posed no inheritance problems. The *investiture* or appointment of the clerical princes had begun.

Otto I reverted to Charlemagne's borderland policy. He installed Count

ist as a political unit. The dukedoms remained fully independent. All Henry I's great achievements were carried out by him as the Duke of Saxony. The doctrines of Christ and the Church, in a simple, childish translation, had by now reached the hearts of German peasants and burghers, alongside the cruelty, barbary and roughness of the times. An intense piety and strong belief were searching for forceful expression.

The Carolingian era had consisted mainly of imitation of the superficially-understood doctrine of antiquity, mingled with the memory of the distant Germanic past. The Romanesque, with its weighty, stereometric structures, the powerful naves, the square towers and round arches, the majestic Madonnas, the triumphant representations of Christ the King and the naive epic frescoes, bronze tableaux of the porches and stone door-panels (tympana), depicting the triumph and judgment of the ruler of the world—all this was a younger German art form. This collection and early form of German being had its beginnings under Henry I and developed splendidly under the following Saxon emperors, the Ottonians.

It was significant for the now con-

Gero to guard the central Elbe region and carry the imperial banner against the Slavs; Bohemia also had to acknowledge the supremacy of the Germans once more. But Otto was not content simply to force the borderland peoples into submission. He tried to convert them to Christianity and win them over to the Empire.

Castles, monasteries and churches were built, the dioceses of Havelberg, Brandenburg, Merseburg, Zeitz (later Naumberg) and Meissen were founded. The newly-won eastern territory was governed from the archbishopric of Magdeburg. In the north the dioceses of Schleswig, Aarhus and Ripen were established. As political units, the three *margravedoms* of Nordmark, Lausitz and Meissen emerged.

At last, Germany seemed to have become a powerful reality. This was shown when the old enemy, the Hungarian cavalry, again attempted to move westwards. The king appeared in 955 with a united army of all the tribes and slaughtered them on the Lechfeld near Augsburg.

In the tracks of the fleeing Hungarians, a wave of Bavarian colonization swept down the Danube, as it had previously done during the time of Tassilo. The Eastern Marches once more became part of Bavaria, and before the end of the century, Stephen the Holy, married to Henry of Bavaria's granddaughter, achieved victory in the land of the Hungarians.

The papacy was at this time in a desolate state. Noble Roman families, emancipated women, such as Theodora and Marozia, were vying with each other for pre-eminence in the Church State, and laying claim to the papal throne. The Italian land which had been won with the spear, fell into the hands of regional "kings." In response to the Pope's appeal for aid, Otto I arrived with the mighty German army, restored order, and was crowned Emperor in Rome by the Pope in 962.

The "Holy Roman Empire," led by the "German nation" arose as a new entity and comprised almost the whole of central Europe, from Jutland as far as southern Italy. In order to reconcile the western crown of the Empire with the eastern one of the "Second Rome" in Byzantium (Constantinople), Otto I married his son Otto II to Theophano, the daughter of Emperor Romano II.

Otto II, the successor, was eighteen years old when the great Emperor went to his grave. He had unceasingly to defend all that his father had achieved. While his court blossomed with the spirit of Greece—an influence brought to the west by his wife Theophano—his cousin, Henry the

Quarrelsome of Bavaria, rose up against him, in an attempt to win Swabia for himself. When the Bavarian was defeated, the marches of Verona and Kärnten were taken from him and made into dukedoms. Luitpold of Babenberg was given the eastern march as an independent *margravedom*. Then Italy called upon the young king to put a stop to rebel Greeks and Arabs who wanted to separate the southern regions, where-

upon Otto went triumphantly to Tarent. Then he called the German and Italian princes to a parliament at Verona. It was there that he first heard of the massive uprising of the Slavs: the open borders to the north were casting their shadow on the construction of the Empire. A few years previously Otto II had already had to defend Lorraine against an attack from the French king, and free the imperial city of Aachen. Churches between the

Oder and the Elbe were burning, the Slavs were rushing in. All this news so shook the twenty-eight-year-old Emperor that he caught a fever in Rome and died.

The heir to the throne was three years old. First, the clever, highly-educated Theophano reigned on behalf of her son Otto III—a role in which she was later followed by his grandmother Adelheid. Both women were supported by the Archbishop of

sionary, had become a martyr at the hands of the heathen Prussians. Gnesen became an archbishopric and the first mission center of Poland. In Aachen Otto III opened up Charlemagne's tomb, so that he could look his great predecessor in the face.

Next he made a pilgrimage to Rome, because, in the atmosphere of exalted religious sentiment characteristic of the age, it was commonly thought that the end of the world and the Day of Judgment would both come in the year 1,000. While he was living in a cave as a hermit and preparing to meet his Redeemer, Italy was in revolt. When he hurried to Rome—fulfilling the fate of many emperors and indicating what was to come for many more—he was driven out of the Holy City by rebels. The twenty-two-year-old Otto died within sight of the Roman walls. His body was carried, with an armed escort, through the uproar of Italy to the tomb in Aachen.

The Saxon Dynasty went to the grave with him. However, the way was paved for the future Germans: the fate of the German nation lay between principalities, struggles against neighboring peoples and obligations to the Popes—between the claims of the Empire and those of the Church, between Germany and Italy.

Mainz, Willigis. Again there were uprisings from the Bavarians, the dukes were threatening the imperial power. Italy lapsed into yet another round of internal strife.

When Otto III, educated by Latin and Greek scholars, grew into the "wonder of the world", seemingly capable of taking over the government of the Empire by himself, the young king proved to have the most high-flying plans. Rome was once more to become the central force of the world, the papacy and the Empire were once more to be closely linked: he called upon the strength of the German nation to re-create the defunct Roman Empire. The young Emperor introduced Byzantine ceremony, drew away from German ways and displayed fantastic religious ideas. He went barefoot on a pilgrimage to Gnesen to the grave of his friend Adalbert of Prague, who, as a mis-

2 Emperors and Popes

As the threshold of one thousand years was crossed, things looked good for Europe. This is particularly true if we compare the situation to that around 500, when barbarity, brutality, violence and destruction ruled the scene towards the end of the *Völkerwanderung.*

Now the Christianised German tribes were united after great ruin,

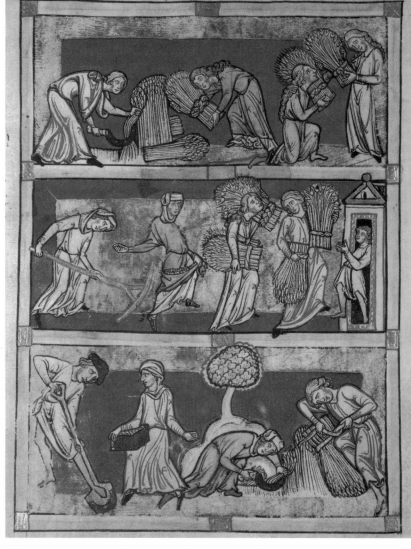

and after detaching themselves from their West Frankish cousins. The borders of the nations were clearly defined, and a mighty empire had arisen, which dreamed of being the successor to the defunct Roman Empire.

Culture, which had sunk into neglect, blossomed forth once more. The court of the Saxon Dynasty was rightly considered the most chaste in Europe:

noble ladies like Theophano and Adelheid were trying to introduce finer customs, learned men from foreign lands came to Germany to practise science and the arts. Even in the newly-founded towns of the north German region, such as Hildesheim, Brunswick, Halberstadt, Magdeburg, Halle, Bremen and Bardewieck, a cultural life emerged, which compared favorably with that in the old Roman towns on the Rhine and Danube, which had now been newly settled once again.

As trade also followed the old Roman paths, from the Rhine and Danube to the Rhone and into Italy, the towns and monasteries which lay along these roads gradually assumed a major economic significance. The *bourgeoisie* grew to the point where it came to acquire an important status in society.

And yet many ancient social forms still remained: the peasants still judged according to old Germanic laws at the "Taiding"; old folk law ruled in the village setting, and even the election of a new king proceeded on the Field of May, following old Germanic tradition.

When, after the end of the Saxon Dynasty, Henry of Bavaria, the founder of the diocese of Bamberg, and sponsor of the monasteries, died, the house of Henry I was finally extinguished.

All the German tribes—princes, Nobles, freemen, assembled near Kamba and Oppenheim, on the right bank of the Rhine, and, by raising their swords and shields, elected the Frankish count Conrad II as the German King. With him the Salian-Frankish house came to the throne for the next hundred years (1024–1125).

As soon as he was elected, Conrad departed with his army of followers to

Italy, to claim the Iron Crown of the Lombards in Milan and the Imperial Crown in Rome. This procedure had by now become a tradition; the close connection between the German rulers and the Roman Popes was newly strengthened. When a German king was sworn in, it was said "may he at all times increase the realm". Conrad fulfilled this aspect of his duties to the German nation. He extended the borders on all sides. His main achievement was to add Burgundy to the empire; Burgundy was a kingdom which stretched from Basle across the Rhone valley, as far as the Mediterranean. The great aim of the Salian king was to increase the power of the realm and empire. This reflected also his personal policy. When the dukes' families in Swabia and Bavaria died out, leaving huge fiefs, he added these to his own family estate; he chose abbots and bishops, installed them on their fiefs, thus making them dependent upon him.

In the meantime the system of mounted followers, which had furthered the aims of the Merovingian kings in France, and Henry I in Saxony, had spread throughout Europe. Everywhere there were knights who ruled over small "under-fiefs" and owed service to their counts, dukes, bishops or abbots. Conrad II now ordered the inheritance of these tiny fiefs. In northern Italy he had to make a special law, because the big "Capitani" did not want to accord this inheritance to their "Valvassoren". The economically and politically weaker peoples, knights, *burghers* and peasants, looked to the Emperor as their protector, to defend their rights against the superior force of princes and land-owners. It was the Emperor who closed the wounds of the Slavs' revolt and forced King Miesco of Po-

land to give up the occupied territories, and obliged him to acknowledge the supremacy of the Empire. And the Emperor also allowed the Norman Rainulf to lay the foundations of a Norman State in Lower Italy. This of course gave rise to a conflict with the Church, wich could and would never allow Upper and Lower Italy to be influenced by one and the same ruler. If this were to happen, the Church State would be completely surrounded and forced into political dependence. The Church also resisted the Emperor in other matters, as he did not shrink from giving away Church dignities along with their appropriate fiefs, and installing and withdrawing bishops as if they were his officials.

In spite of this conflict, Conrad II was a deeply pious man, and laid the foundation stone of Speier Cathedral, later the burial place of the Salian kings.

His son, Henry III (1039–1056) was twenty-two years old when he succeeded to the throne. In contrast to his father, who could neither read nor write, he was highly educated. He too was filled by the conviction of his duty to the Empire, and devoted himself fervently to it.

He forced the Bohemian Duke Bretislav, who hoped to use the fall of the Polish State to found a great Slavonic power, to acknowledge German supremacy; he led the Hungarian king, who had been driven out by heathen enemies, back to his lands, and brought the whole of Lorraine back into the Empire.

In the border provinces, wars, acts of violence and feuds were rampant among the nobles. In the southern French regions the clergy announced a "treuga dei"—Truce of God—in order to interrupt the endless fighting.

Henry III accepted this idea and introduced it for the whole realm: on all holy days, and from Wednesday evening to Monday morning there was to be no fighting or violence. Under Henry III, the voice of the Church, protesting against imperial supremacy and arbitrariness, became louder. This voice came especially from the Burgundian monastery of Cluny, which had formed a "congregation" with numerous other monasteries. The reform-seeking monks of Cluny vociferously opposed marriage for the priesthood, corruption of the high clerics and simoniacal practices.

The Gospel tells of the money-changer Simon, who wanted to buy the power of miracle-working for cash. When the monks of Cluny spoke about simoniacal practices, they meant the trading of offices and Church dignities by holders of worldly power, (such as the Emperor) and the high clerics. Bishoprics and rich monasteries were given away to the posthumous sons of counts and princes, other positions were bought for money. In this way the court chancellery created a good income, but also a group of sure supporters, for an appointment as bishop meant also the endowment of lands and vassals. Henry III himself, at Sutri and Rome, had removed from office three unworthy and troublesome popes, and he had installed the same number of Germans on the throne of St. Peter, with the help of his army. The Cluny movement refused to continue to recognize the Emperor's power of decree over the Church. Basing their argument on the words of Christ: "Here are two swords", the Cluny monks wanted to restrict the Emperor to the exercise of worldly power, and make him leave all spiritual matters to the Pope. And for them, spiritual matters

Below: Emperor Henry IV and the Antipope Clement III chasing Pope Gregory VII from Rome in 1084. In actual fact, Gregory fled to Salerno where he died a year later. From the Ottonian Chronicles, 12th century.

ruled over worldly affairs, just as the realm of God ruled over all people.

However, there was no showdown over these ideas. Henry III met with a fate similar to that of Otto II. At the height of his career, aged only thirty-nine, he had just defeated the Normans in Italy, when two pieces of very grave news were brought to him: the south-German princes had sworn to murder the Emperor, and the Slavonic *Liutiz* army had destroyed a German army. Henry rushed home deeply affected by this news, and died at Bodfelz in the Harz mountains. His heir, Henry IV, was not yet six years old.

Much of what happened next can only be explained by the tempestuous youth of Henry IV. At first his mother Agnes, a weak woman, ruled on his behalf. Immediately, the dukes increased their power. Soon, the ruthless, imperious Archbishop Anno of Cologne became the young king's regent. He reared him in a highly authoritarian way, inflicting corporal punishment upon hin. Anno was obliged to accept his rival, Adalbert of Bremen, as co-regent, and passed the boy-king over to this high-living archbishop. Adalbert tried to win Henry's favor by allowing him complete freedom, declared him of age at 15 years,

and delivered him to the joys of licentious living.

At Goslar Henry surrounded himself with ministers, held drinking parties and orgies, thrust princes, burghers and knights away from him, and treated his bright, faithful wife Bertha as a servant. Full of the arrogance of youth, he then tried to "govern": he was fully convinced of his unique aptitude to be emperor, used the "investiture" to bestow Church offices at random for profit, took away estates from the weaker landowners, and wasted the state's riches on his doubtful friends. Then the Saxons rose up against him and a

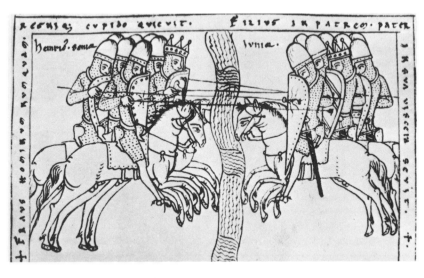

Below: Emperor Henry IV (right) fighting his son Henry V at the battle of Ratisbonne. Fearing that his father's clashes with the Pope might cost him his rights to the imperial throne, Henry V led a conspiracy which forced his father to abdicate, at the Congress of the Princes at Ingelheim (1106).

rebellion drove him from Goslar.

With the help of his princes the young king managed to put down the rebels. Suddenly he seemed to be a real king, and to wield the power of his office.

Then, an opponent of far superior intellect came on the scene and altered everything. The Cluniac monk Hildebrand, who, under Henry III had accompanied the banished Pope Gregory VI into exile at Cologne, and who knew German conditions exactly, was made Pope Gregory VII in 1073. The very fact that he called himself Gregory VII was a challenge to the Emperor, because, according to the

Emperor there had never been a Gregory VI.

The Cluny movement had for a long time been preaching against "lay investiture", that is, the holding of Church offices by princes or emperors. This sentiment was strongly echoed among the population of the northern-Italian towns, which had recently acquired a new sense of awareness, and which, moreover, had similar problems. The prosperous, obstinate *bourgeoisie*, struggling to govern themselves, refused to accept the rule of the Emperor's chosen "podestas". The time was ripe for demanding more freedom, greater rights of contribution, and independence from the Emperor's power.

At a fasting synod in Rome, Pope Gregory VII dared to forbid investiture and challenge the Empire to battle.

Being completely ignorant of the spiritual change which the people had meanwhile undergone, due to the unremitting efforts of the monks and lower clergy, Henry believed that he could answer the Pope arrogantly and scornfully. He addressed his message

to "Hildebrand, not the Pope, but a false monk", and relied on the argument that he had the German army against the Pope's ideological power. Gregory reacted with an unusual weapon: he excommunicated Henry and his followers, deposed him from his office, and released his subjects from their oath of allegiance.

Being banned from the Church and cursed by St Peter's successor had an enormous effect on all pious, naive minds on the other side of the Alps. First, princes and bishops left the King's army, then the knights and servants defected. The Saxons rose up again; only a few sympathetic towns on the Rhine remained faithful to the King.

Meanwhile the Pope and the German princes had declared that if, within a year, the excommunication was not lifted, the King would lose his crown. The Pope had already been invited to Augsburg to preside over the choosing of a successor. Now the consequences were becoming evident: it was clear that, as the Pope had bestowed the crown of the Roman Empire on Charlemagne—he could also

23

take it away from Charlemagne's successor. In that unusually severe winter, when the Rhine froze over, the wolves roamed around outside the town walls, and the vine-roots froze, Henry IV and his wife Bertha, in Speier, went through the worst crisis of their lives. During these frozen months Henry IV changed into a politician and ruler. He understood which way he had to go.

Forsaken by everyone, the King travelled with his wife and year-old son, Henry V, up the Rhine in a sled; helped by huntsmen and shepherds he crossed over the Alpine peaks in midwinter, because the Bavarian passes were barred by hostile princes; he finally reached the Plain of Lombardy in the early spring of 1077. Here he proved that he had become a mature politician. At the news of the Emperor's appearance, the "podestas" and mighty "capitani" of northern Italy assembled to offer him support and to rise with him against the Pope; for the nobility were just as unhappy about the "*Pataria movement*" in the towns as they were about the Cluniac preaching of freedom and right of contribution. Henry IV, however, realised that the strength of the Empire lay not with the Italian vassals, but solely with the German tribes, Hed had to win these back to his side, even if it meant submission and penance.

Pope Gregory VII (already en route for Augsburg), heard of the King's arrival, thought that he must have brought an army, and fled to Canossa Castle, which belonged to his friend, Matilda of Tuscany. The German King and Emperor-designate arrived there dressed in penitent's clothing, and begged forgiveness. Gregory the politician would have liked to refuse him this license to re-

newed activity, but as a priest he could not. To him the German king was no more than a repentant lamb returning to Christ's flock. After three days of humiliating waiting in the courtyard of Castle Canossa, Henry IV was granted audience, his confession heard, and he was admitted to Communion, thereby being released from his excommunication.

Everything had changed: The King returned to his empire. He had fulfilled the condition, and he called upon his supporters, most of whom obeyed the command. His enemies produced an anti-king, but the King's side defeated them at the first clash of arms. Then Henry went seeking vengeance to Italy and Rome. He found the Holy City in a state of disruption and the Pope had fled. Henry quickly chose an anti-pope, Clement III, who solemnly crowned him Roman Emperor at St. Peter's.

Church laws already existed, according to which only a synod of selected bishops and archbishops had the right to elect the new Pope. These Church "princes" were later to be known by the Latin name "cardo", hence the cardinals of the Church.

Once more the Emperor had invested a Pope, while Gregory VII sat powerless in his fortress, the Castle of Sant' Angelo. Shortly before the Emperor's entry into Italy, Gregory VII had recognised the southern-Italian Norman state of Robert Guiscard as a feudal Church State. Now the Normans came to his aid and the German army had to retreat. The Normans plundered and ravaged Rome, and as they marched away they took the Pope, by now cursed by the whole of Rome, with them. The great Gregory died in exile on Monte Cassino in 1085.

In Germany the civil war of the princes had begun. The Crusades had got underway, the political power of Rome had increased, and the Emperor once more found himself excommunicated. Various factions were fighting in all regions of the Empire. When Henry finally seemed to be in sight of peace, around the turn of the century, his own son, Henry V, rose up against him, took him prisoner, and at the Diet of Ingelheim in 1105, forced him to abdicate. He died at Liège one year later. His body had to wait five years in an unconsecrated chapel of Speier Cathedral, before he was granted absolution, and could be buried in the imperial vault of the Salians. Fifteen years later Henry V succeeded in resolving the tiresome investiture dispute by the Concordat of Worms (1122). This proclaimed that Church dignitaries would from now on be invested by the Pope, who would give them the ring and crozier, but that the King would bestow their temporal power by the touch of his sceptre.

The Papacy had asserted its spiritual omnipotence over the sword of the Emperor. From now on two powers laid rival claims to the government of Europe.

The Holy Roman Empire of the German nation had, of course, emerged weakened from this struggle, which had ravaged its regions during two generations; moreover, its end also marked the end of the Frankish-Salian house.

The struggle between the Empire and the Papacy, between the temporal and spiritual realms, produced an impassioned response throughout the Western world; indeed, it came to permeate every aspect of life for vast numbers of people.

Asceticism and hedonism, wealth and evangelical poverty, self-sacrifice in the pursuit of high ideals or sheer adventure, mysticism and realism—all of these elements combined to form the splendidly colorful picture of the advancing Middle Ages; it was a picture which later ages took to represent the highest form of achievement and an unattainable goal.

Cathedrals reached up from the dark streets to Heaven. Castles and fortresses crowned the mountain peaks; in the rose gardens of Provence the songs of knightly troubadours could be heard, the monasteries resounded to the melancholy hymns of the Cistercian monks, and the great schools of the West beamed forth the spirit of scholasticism.

In the days around the turn of the century, as Germany was torn by the civil war of the tribes and the princes, the call to the Crusades could be heard. The Western world was being summoned to free the tomb of the Redeemer from the hands of Islam, and to re-establish the old Empire on the ancient Christian soil of Syria and Palestine.

This incitement of the feelings to acts of faith, to the adventure of richly-rewarded conquests, had been felt in Franconia, Burgundy, Italy, and along the lower Rhine. Papal policy strengthened the western princes in their undertaking, because, once the main part of the fighting forces had departed to the Orient, it would be easier for the Church to strengthen her own rule throughout the provinces.

In Germany the call to the Crusades, following as it did on the investiture dispute and internal struggles, was at first taken up only along the Rhine. A wild, rootless gathering of knights, servants and adventurers set out. As there were no heathens or heretics in their own land, on whom they could give vent to their strength and aggression, the wrath of the people turned against the only non-Christians, they knew, the hated Jewish minority. Ever since Otto II's time, these eternal wanderers had had the right to settle in ghettos in shady parts of the towns. However, as they were not allowed to own land, and were not accepted in Christian guilds, fellowships or societies, they were, from the very beginning, condemned to follow that trade which was forbidden to the Christians by Church law; the trade of money-lending and tax-collecting.

Many patricians, counts, princes, knights and burghers were in debt to the Jewish money-lenders. If they could kill them, many financial concerns would be dissolved. Thus the first wave of crusaders rushed murdering and burning through the Jewish quarters. The authorities, for obvious reasons, hardly intervened. In the winter of the year 1100, the Rhine near Speier was blocked with Jewish corpses.

The Jewish pogrom gripped the whole of Europe: Franconia, Burgundy, the Low Countries and England. Only the King of Poland offered asylum to these persecuted people, because he needed efficient traders, laborers and learned people for his land. Thus in murder and violence the basis was established for that eastern Jewry which centuries later streamed back across the German borders.

It was only Second Crusade, announced in a fiery speech by Bernard of Clairvaux before Conrad III and the German princes in Speier Cathedral, which inspired the Germans to take part, with an imposing army.

In the Orient, thrown together with nobles and knights from all different regions and provinces, the knights felt

the need to distinguish themselves from each other. They began to paint pictures on their shields, pictures which developed into coats of arms. The name of one's place of origin was added to the Christian name as a distinguishing mark: knight Kuno from Felseneck called himself Kuno von Felseneck, in order to distinguish

himself from Kuno von Greifenstein.

There, in the south and the east, the Germans came into contact with a higher culture and civilization than their own. At the Saracen courts they learned the attraction of *"Höflichkeit"* (courtly manners), good table manners, the service of ladies, verse-writing and singing; they copied the Arabs' mounted game, their "*turnu*", and so came to love the jousting tournament. But the contact with learned Greeks and Orientals opened up for them many new ideas and concepts, which they called by the Greek word "*Katharern*", which developed into the German "*Ketzertum*"—heresy. From the Moorish schools of Andalusia, but also directly from the Orient, the knowledge of algebra, alchemy, world geography, medicine and other sciences now came to the lands of the Danube and Rhine.

In the waters of Kiel the crusading armies sailed and rowed in the ships of the Italian coastal towns, such as Amalfi, Genoa, Pisa and Venice. The old trading train of ancient history, which had followed the "mare nostrum" and exchanged the goods of the Western world for the spices, gold and dyes of the east, now opened up once more the ruined paths of the Roman Empire.

At first it was only the Italian markets and trading posts which experienced the flourishing new trade; but soon the paths of the merchants followed the old Roman roads to the north—from the Rhone, across Burgundy as far as the Rhine, from Genoa, Florence and Venice, through Milan and Verona to the Alpine passes and up to Augsburg, Ulm, Regensburg and Nuremberg. The towns grew and flourished.

Since trade necessitated the common denominator of money, the economic system switched from a north-south basis to an east-west one, and from a barter to a cash economy.

The feudal system was based on the ownership of land. The lord of the manor's power lay in his vassals and feudal tenure. The emperor's income was all in the form of goods—a system which had given rise to the landed nobility and the knights. Now, however, money gained in significance, soon came the "Lombardic exchange", credit, and coins made from precious metals. The ownership of land no longer counted as much as money, the emphasis was transferred from the country to the towns, from the knight to the *burgher*.

The Emperor, who was assigned vassals, fiefs and goods, was soon to stand opposed to the growing self-awareness of the towns and princes, who were supported by the power of money and the direct taxation of their subjects.

The world of the Germans suddenly opened up to further possibilities; the hitherto largely agricultural structure quickly changed to a system of limited world trade and an early form of capitalism. The Church, as a primarily spiritual power, soon adapted itself to the altered circumstances: it was no longer just Peter's pennies and *Palliengeld* (to be paid at the investiture of all high clergy), which filled her coffers; the Church also founded banks and held out her hands for donations, penance-money, and finally indulgences. She became a financial power.

Now more than ever ensnared in the web of ancient feudalism, the German Empire hardly had the power to bridge the gap over into the new times. At the peak of its history, under the glorious house of Hohenstaufen (1138–1254), the Empire was fighting a desperate battle against the new times.

27

3 The Hohenstaufen Empire

After the death of Henry V (1125), the fate of the Empire once more lay in the hands of the German princes. Under the Frankish-Salian emperors, something resembling the hereditary succession of a dynasty had developed. Now, however, as the direct line of this house had died out, and the feeling of aversion to the authoritarian reign of Henry V had reached a climax, the rulers of the German provinces chose for their new king not the next in line, Henry's nephew Duke Frederick of Swabia, but Lothar, Duke of Saxony. The Swabian dukes, who were called by the name of their native castle of Hohenstaufen, refused to yield up the imperial fiefs, so Lothar, along with his son-in-law Henry the Proud of Bavaria, declared war on them, and the two noble houses of the Hohenstaufens and the Welfs, though closely related, became deadly enemies. Fratricidal wars raged in southern Germany and northern Italy, until Lothar, on one of his Italian campaigns, finally succeeded in getting himself crowned Emperor by the Pope. The feud between the Hohenstaufens and the Welf-Saxons was therefore decided in favor of the latter, and Lothar acquired great power in Germany.

The new Emperor used this power to continue the work of Germanizing and Christianizing the lands between the Baltic Sea and the rivers Elbe and Oder. The Marches of Meissen were given over to Conrad of Wettin, whilst the Northern Marchlands were given to Count Albrecht "the Bear". This latter relative of the Welfs quickly extended his territory as far as the Havel and Spree rivers to found the Marches of Brandenburg, and then beyond the Oder he founded the New Marches. Between the lower Elbe and Oder

only the Slavonic *Obotrits* in Mecklenburg resisted him. Even in Polish territory in Pomerania and in Upper Silesia, Bishop Otto of Bamberg was preaching the Christian doctrine. It was especially the new orders of the Cistercians and Premonstratensians, which had both evolved from the Clunian movement, who went east at the Polish rulers' bidding, to do the same work in the Slavonic territory as Boniface had done among the wild Germanic tribes four hundred years before. The monks founded monasteries and churches, led convoys of Franconian, Saxon and Frisian settlers into the land, where they began to drain swamps, clear forests and build villages. Up until this time the Slavs had avoided freeing the protective wall of the Slovakian Ore Mountains and the Sudetes from their thick forests, and land-seekers from Thuringia, Franconia, and Bavaria now rushed in to settle there. In Silesia, the Polish *piastre* dukes called upon the skilful Germans to deliver the country from the primitive agriculture of the Slavonic *opol* peasants and bring it to fruition. A new wave of eastwards migration set in, but this time it was no disorderly departure of unruly masses, but a planned and ordered emigration of large and small groups from the Empire.

At first this whole operation was led by the lords of the manor, the Cistercian monasteries and other clerical land-owners; later the business was transferred to wealthy managers, called *"locators"*: as room for settlement had become scarce in the western part of the Empire, and the surplus population was clamoring for land, many peasants, laborers and knights moved into the newly-opened-up eastern territory. The Germans settled as free men, while the "locator" *"heißt ihnen*

29

Tannhäuser, the famous ·
minnesinger, or lyric poet, of the
13th century, shown here with the
crusader's cloak.

lediglich die Schuld''—that is, he collected the rent for the land-owner, an office which developed into that of *"Schultheiss"* or village mayor. Through Christianization, colonization and hard work, the young provinces of Pomerania, Neumark, Silesia and the Sudetenland therefore leaned heavily towards the Empire.

After the death of Lothar of Saxonia in 1137, the dispute between the Hohenstaufens and the Welfs flared up again. Henry of Bavaria, Emperor Lothar's son-in-law had been given the rich estates of Matilda of Italy, but also the dukedom of Saxony, so he laid claim to the throne. Out of envy and fear of Henry the Proud, the assembly of German princes were moved to elect his opponent, Conrad of Hohenstaufen. Now the Hohenstaufens were hitting back. The new king, Conrad III, gave Bavaria to Leopold of Austria, and Saxony to Albrecht the Bear; he kept the Italian imperial fiefs for himself. The Welfs rose up, and the cry of "Welf: Waibling: (Hohenstaufen)" could be heard in numerous feuds throughout southern Germany. The main problem of the Empire was obvious—that in fact this empire and the German nation were simply an idea, that they were not a living reality. The whole scene was dominated by noble houses, all seeking to strengthen their own power, as well as by tribal feuds and the question of land ownership—, but certainly not by any imperial policy. The King and Emperor was simply the first of these nobles, and was only as powerful as the strength of his own house. Peasants and burghers alike were caught helplessly between the feuds of the princes, who had troops of knights to fight for them.

This inner strife could be seen most clearly of all in the Italian part of the

The instruments most typical
of the Middle Ages – a choir organ,
a cornet, a hurdy-gurdy and
a carillon.

Empire. The rapid growth of the trading posts in Lombardy and the newly-won riches of Mediterranean trade and a money-based economy, led the *bourgeoisie* to reassert its self-awareness, and everywhere, from the craftsmen's guilds to the great patrician families, even among the simplest peasants, the *Pataria* movement was giving rise to a revolutionary spirit. The guilds demanded to be allowed to take part in local government, native merchants and patricians demanded the right to be master in their own house. The time was coming to an end when imperial "podestas" could rule arbitrarily over land "won by the spear". As the Popes, in Italy, were resisting the omnipotence of

Germany and the Emperor, these factions from the towns united with the Church and also with the Welfs, who were still struggling against the Hohenstaufen emperor. But the Empire also had its partisans: land-owners of Germanic origin, knightly *valvassors*, powerful *capitani*, and wealthy merchants, to whom the order and peace of central Europe was more important than local self-government, and who had close business and trade links with the north. The one side of the struggle called itself the "Guelfs", after the Welfs in its ranks, and the others were known as the "Ghibellines". The battle raged in the streets of Lombardic and Tuscan towns, in the country, over half of Italy.

When Conrad committed the political folly of allowing the fighting force of the Empire to embark upon a Crusade at this time of internal conflict, the confusion increased. Conrad died just as his cousin, Henry the Lion, a Welf, had begun to fight over Bavaria (1152).

In Frankfurt the German princes elected as his successor his nephew, the young, arrogant Frederick of Hohenstaufen, Duke of Swabia. He was crowned Frederick I (1152–1190) in Aachen. This young, educated man was filled with the most exalted ideas about the Empire and the role of Emperor. He cherished the dream of a Universal Empire, of an ordered, Christian Western World ruled over

by the crown of the Caesars. He had been brought up in the "seven devotions" of knighthood, but his knowledge and education went far beyond these. His friends were travelling poets, courtly singers, historians and philosophers such as Otto of Freising. The Italians called him Barbarossa, because of his red beard; peoples, princes and even his enemies admired him and were filled with respect for this man who tried to rule strictly and justly.

First of all he tried to find a settlement in Germany by giving back to his cousin, Henry the Lion, not only Saxony, but also Bavaria; he even gave the Italian imperial fiefs to a Welf. Austria was separated from Bavaria and became an independent dukedom.

Once he had won peace there, he applied himself to the true imperial task, and left for Italy, to establish the Empire's diminished power there again. In this undertaking, which had led mighty German armies to Italy five times in the last twenty years, Frederick Barbarossa showed that his elevated ideas and aspirations belonged to a past which could not be resurrected.

Followed by a doubtful band of supporters, his princes and their knights, and with no understanding of the fervent, democratic, national movement in the Lombardic towns, he took up the fight against a Church which had an army of a hundred thousand monkish zealots, and against the burghers who had their coffers full of cash.

In the meantime, many Lombardic towns had cast aside the old laws of the bishops and counts, had mounted civil guards, bought influential *capitani* as their allies, and elected civic consuls and judges. In Rome, as a re-

sult of fiery sermons from a reformer called Arnold of Brescia, a "Roman republic" had evolved. Even smaller towns had declared themselves "free communes".

However, Frederick succeeded in taking Rome, having himself crowned Emperor, and Arnold of Brescia burned at the stake, but he failed to overcome the power of Milan. He rushed back to Germany, arranged new deals with the princes, married Beatrice of Burgundy and put down a Slavonic revolt in Poland and Silesia. Rainald von Dassel became his chan-

cellor, Count Otto of Wittelsbach his closest friend. Once more he returned to Italy, this time forcing Milan to submit, and dismissed his army of knights, who were impatient to go home. He held a parliament with his princes in the fields near Verona, where he re-established the principles of the *Codex Justinianus* and his imperial rights (regalia). The old, medieval feudal system was to be re-introduced. But this was too much: the proud city of Milan again rose against him, only to be defeated yet again, and razed to the ground. The consuls had to humble themselves before the Emperor. *Podestas*—imperial governors—were again installed in the Italian towns.

The Pope, who had nothing to gain by the Emperor's supremacy, trampled on this plan. The popes now conveniently espoused the cause of civil liberty, and encouraged the Lombards' resistance to the Emperor, entering into a close alliance with William the Norman, whose territory lay to the south of the Church State. When Pope Adrian died, there was a double election, in which the Emperor's party lost. At the Diet of Besançon the domineering Alexander III cursed the Emperor and threatened him with excommunication, then, in defiance, he had the north-Italian stronghold of Alexandria built. The rebel towns were once more filled with hope, and joined together in the Veronese Alliance. Frederick Barbarossa came over the Alps with a new army of knights and marched into Rome to find the Pope and his cardinals fleeing for their lives.

Then an epidemic broke out in the Holy City, killing thousands of the victorious army: Rainald von Dassel, the brilliant, faithful chancellor, went to his grave, as did many of the German princes. The rest of the army broke up and went back across the Alps in small groups. Milan and its allies then joined up with the Veronese Alliance, and once more raised the banner of rebellion. Alone and forsaken, Frederick Barbarossa made his way back over the Alpine passes, narrowly escaping his enemies' numerous traps.

In Germany the Emperor's most powerful supporter, Henry the Lion, had meanwhile been carrying out his own personal policy, directed at the east of the Empire, and aiming to

strengthen his Saxon dukedom. He had relentlessly extended his rule to include Mecklenburg and part of Pomerania, torn lands away from his neighbors, and stirred up a whole union of north-German princes against him. The Emperor, on his return home, had to make the peace. He sided with his obstinate cousin and allowed him to form his own realm within the Empire—from Lübeck to Saxony, across Bavaria as far as Tuscany.

The Emperor needed Henry's help for his fifth Italian campaign, but Henry refused to support him, as he could and would not leave his stolen lands in northern Germany unprotected. So a small German army was utterly defeated by the superior forces of the Lombards in May 1176.

At last Frederick understood that he had lost the battle of knightly swords against rich money-coffers, that he had lost the war between national, civil freedom and the imperial system of government. In Venice, under humiliating conditions, he made his peace with the Pope and the Lombards. While proud patricians and their ladies looked down from the galleries of the Doge's Palace, Frederick held the Pope's stirrup and kissed his foot.

The Emperor, now old and grey, returned once more over the Alps, to settle accounts with his faithless supporter, Henry the Lion. At the parliament of Würzburg, Henry was banished and divested of all his estates. Bavaria, apart from a small dukedom, was ceded to the Emperor's friend, Otto of Wittelsbach, while Saxony was divided up among the heirs of Albrecht the Bear and the neighboring princes. Only later, when Henry the Lion had humbled himself, did his family at long last receive back their

inherited lands of Brunswick and Limburg.

At last there was peace in the Empire. At Mainz, Frederick Barbarossa celebrated at Whitsuntide in 1184 with great tournaments and knightly festivities, when his sons Frederick and Henry were given their swords; this was one of the most glorious medieval pageants, sung about by the courtly poet Henry of Veldecke. When Frederick Barbarossa now went to Italy for the sixth time, he went in peace as the undisputed Emperor. In Milan—now rebuilt and reconciled—he celebrated the magnificent wedding of his son Henry, to Constance, the heir to the kingdom of "both Sicilies". The Norman realm therefore now came within the sphere of German power. This, of course, was a source of concern and anger for the Pope, who now saw his Church State surrounded and caught up within the grasp of the same power. Thus the news of the fall of Jerusalem came at a favorable time for Rome: it was a good opportunity to send the too-powerful Emperor to the Orient with his army. The old Emperor set off, leading a most glorious army of knights to the east; he wanted to be true to the duty of the Caesars, the Protector of Christendom and the strongarm of the Church. He never returned. On 10th June 1190 he was drowned in the river Selef.

Under Barbarossa's son and successor, Henry VI (1190–1197), the medieval empire of the Germans reached its peak and achieved its greatest expansion. In contrast to his father, Henry VI was a young, aggressive, cruel, extremely hard and greedy man, gripped by something approaching Caesarian delusions. Once he had pacified Henry the Lion, who had returned from his English exile,

The Dominican Albert the Great (about 1193–1280) or Albert of Bollstadt was one of the great masters of the Middle Ages. One of his disciples was Thomas of Aquinas.

and made sure of the safety of the German nucleus, he went to Italy, had himself crowned Emperor, and threw his weight relentlessly against southern Italy and Sicily. The Norman line of succession had been extinguished there. Henry claimed the inheritance in the name of his wife, Constance. Using torture, executions, terror and violence, he made his way to Palermo, where he claimed the Norman crown. As he had now inherited both the Norman territory and the Crusade, his power now reached out to Tunisia, Greece, Cyprus, and even as far as the Syrian dominions between Aleppo and the Lebanon.

When the English King Richard the Lionheart, on his way home from the Crusades, fell into the hands of his arch-enemy, Leopold of Austria, and was delivered up to the Emperor, Henry was able to force the English King to acknowledge the feudal majesty of the Empire, and to agree to unite parts of the Anglo-Norman navy with the imperial fleets of Genoa, Amalfi, Sicily and the united fleets of Venice, the Pope and the Byzantine Emperor.

Confronted with such awesome authority, the Spanish kings of Aragon and Leon-Castile acknowledged the feudal sovereignty of the Empire, and even the French king took the expansion of the Germano-Roman Empire seriously.

The time seemed to have come when the ancient Roman Empire would be revived by German strength. A mighty Crusade was to gather half of Europe's knights in Messina and lead to a decisive thrust to the east. When Rome's Christian provinces in Syria and Egypt were won back, the "mare nostrum" (the Mediterranean) would once more become the sea of history, the trading

The grandson of Frederick I Barbarossa, Frederick II, made one last attempt to make the universal empire a reality. He made Sicily one of the most modern states in Europe at that time.

route of nations, and the nucleus of a newly-arisen empire.

Shortly before they were to set off, when all preparations had been made, Henry VI rode out to hunt in the swamps near Catania, caught malaria, and died at the age of twenty-three in Messina. The heir to the greatest empire in medieval history was a boy of two-and-a-half years, who was named after his grandfather, Frederick. Pope Innocent III became his guardian; he was reared by kind-hearted nobles, burghers and fishermen of Palermo. At the Norman court he learned all the wisdom of the Saracens, Greeks, Italians and northern peoples; from the fishermen in the port, the traders and bazaar merchants he learned all the cunning of the ancient southern civilization. But he hardly nourished the intention of ever gaining the Norman crown, or even the dukedom of

Swabia, his native seat. He was an abandoned orphan, and a pawn on the chequer-board of politics.

After the death of the severe Emperor, Germany fell into chaos. The Hohenstaufen party elected Philip of Swabia, the Welfs chose the son of Henry the Lion, Otto IV. Once Philip had been murdered, Otto marched with a strong army against Italy and the Pope. This Welf, who was more than six feet tall, was an uncouth barbarian from the north; his seething army behaved like conquerors and overlords. This happened at a time and place filled with the call to reform, with national and libertarian ideas. Francis of Assisi and his beggar-monks were preaching ancient Christian modesty; intensification, simple poverty, respect for all life, mercy, and the precedence of the Christian spirit over earthly power. Two different worlds came face to face. The Pope, who had just crowned Otto IV Emperor, now excommunicated him, and as the German went plundering forth into the Norman kingdom, the Pope remembered the little child of Palermo, on whose shoulders the whole prestige of the Hohenstaufens now rested. Supported by the Pope, Frederick II now arrived on the scene.

The Hohenstaufen king, wretched, without riches, and with very few knights, arrived in his territory along the Upper Rhine. The Welfs called him "*Pfaffenkönig*" (the Pope's king), his supporters hailed him as a second "Barbarossa" and dreamed of the splendor of the Empire. One of these dreamers was Walther von der Vogelweide, who wrote exultant songs in honor of Frederick.

The Germans were chiefly historical dreamers. They assembled in their masses under the Hohenstaufen banner, and crowned Frederick II in

Mainz. Frederick formed an alliance with the Bavarian Wittelsbach house and gave them the Rhine Palatinate as a fief, so that from now on there were two branches to the Wittelsbach house. In the meantime the French king had defeated King John of England and his ally Otto IV at the Battle of Bouvines (1214); this was an event which considerably weakened the Welf king's position. Thus, lucky breaks and the summons of the Hohenstaufen house brought Frederick II to power. Of course, this power was no longer that of Barbarossa. Both Philip and Frederick himself had considerably reduced the size of the realm by bribing the princes; the princes' power had increased throughout the provinces, and although Frederick tried to create a counter-weight by granting many towns the freedom of the Empire, he failed to strengthen his own power; for although the towns were mostly faithful to the Emperor, they pursued realistic policies, largely to their own advantage: inside the towns were tradesmen, merchants, perceptive burghers and money-bags.

In order to placate the Pope, who had made him King and Emperor, Frederick had to acknowledge the feudal supremacy of the Church over his Norman kingdom in southern Italy, renounce his right to take part in the election of the higher clergy, and swear to take part in a Crusade. The Church had the Emperor in its power.

At the Lateran Council of 1215, two new orders of preachers and monks were sanctioned—the Franciscans and the Dominicans; the Inquisition, the Church's protective organization against heresy, was entrusted to the Dominicans, and the State was authorized to undertake the punishment, torture and execution of

Various imperial orders (counts, barons, principal and secondary towns) with their coats of arms and their ceremonial dress.

heretics. Frederick had to enact these laws. In almost the whole of the Western World, the Inquisition Councils now began to meet, ancient Roman tortures were re-introduced as a method of finding out the truth, and the fires of the stake were kindled. Only the German peoples resisted it. The detested heresy-judge Conrad of Marburg wanted to introduce these methods in Germany, but was murdered by a conspiracy of nobles. The Inquisition did not take hold in German lands.

Only when the princes' territorial powers were at stake did violence hide behind the heresy laws. When the free peasants' union from Stedinger on the river Hunte rose up against the infringements of the Archbishop of Bremen and the Count of Oldenburg, they were all declared heretics and destroyed by an army of "Crusaders".

It was also the crusading spirit which led Frederick to command his friend and confidant, Hermann von Salza, to lead his Teutonic Knights—a monastic order of knights—to Transylvania, and later to west and east Prussia, in order to convert the Prussians, Kashubs and Letto-Lithuanians to Christianity, and bring them into the Empire.

Along the Baltic coast there arose a new area of colonization, stretching from the mouth of the Oder to the Gulf of Finland.

Frederick II, who spoke only broken German, but excellent Norman, Arabic, Greek, Latin and French, came from the southern-Italian Norman kingdom. He returned there to find his roots and regain his strength. And so he left Germany, which was degenerating into chaos with feuds, vehmic courts, struggles between the princes, and provincial and internecipe quarrels, to his son Henry, and tried to reconstruct the Empire from Italy.

Pope Gregory IX obliged him to go on a Crusade, so as to divert the Emperor's power; he also excommunicated him, and declared open war on the troublesome southern-Italian realm.

Once more, a conspiracy of self-seeking German princes, the freedom-seeking Lombardic towns, and the spiritual-propagandist strength of the Church united together against the Emperor and his realm. He rushed back from the Holy Land, where he had succeeded in concluding a peace settlement, thanks to his connections with the Saracens. He took up the multiple battle in Italy, which had by now become further complicated by a local struggle between the Guelfs and the Ghibellines, and by intrigues with the Lombards and the Church. In the midst of these protracted wars and struggles, which were never really decisive, Frederick II constructed his "model empire" in southern Italy. This was to be the nucleus and model for a bold new imperial structure, a concept of the State, such as was not seen again until the age of Absolutism.

With his faithful Saracen troops, the Emperor created a standing army,

36

concentrated around a system of fortresses; paid officials administered the country on modern lines, using the taxation system to lay the financial foundation of a centrally-governed state. Surrounded by learned, free-thinking, tolerant people, Frederick sponsored the founding of high schools, such as the Faculty of Medicine at Salerno. He had friends among the Arabs, Scots, Frenchmen, Germans and Greeks; the troubadour poetry of the Romance languages flourished at his court. This court was so free and oriental in its attitude, that many pious people reproached him for his "harem", his Saracen friends,

and his public speeches and writings. Frederick paid little attention to the German part of his empire. He knew nothing of the great poetry of Walther von der Vogelweide, nothing of the minstrels' quarrel at Wartburg, nothing of Wolfram von Eschenbach and other poets of the German language. Wherever it was possible, and where wealth and confederacy made it appropriate, he endowed upon towns, abbeys and noblemen the charters giving freedom of the "Reich". In 1241 he received a strange letter from the Great Khan of the Mongols, who had set out in the tracks of Ghengis Khan, and was marching towards the west with enormous armies. Frederick loved falconry, and hat written a book about it; the Great Khan wanted to employ him to work as chief falconer at his court, as long as he would subject himself. At the same time news arrived of three separate waves of cavalry, who were making their way across Russia and the Balkans towards the borders of the empire, with no-one able to resist them. The western world was in great danger of being overrun by this mighty, inexhaustible storm from the east.

The Emperor could do nothing. He was struggling with all his strength in Italy against the Pope and the Lombardic towns. So the whole burden of defense lay with a 3000-strong army of knights, which Duke Henry of Liegnitz assembled in Silesia. This small body of men were defeated on the Plain of Walstatt in April 1241. Europe lay wide open to the Mongolian attack, and was only saved by the timely death, in remote Karakoram, of the Great Khan himself—a lucky coincidence, which sent all the military leaders rushing back to try to have themselves made Great Khan; to this remarkable stroke of good fortune the

Western World owes its continuation.

The dispute with the Lombards and the Pope became grimmer. At the Diet of Lyons in 1245 the excommunication was renewed and all nations were called upon to fight against the Emperor. Germany elected an anti-king. Frederick was surrounded by treachery and intrigue, his troops suffered defeats, his son Henry, who had betrayed him, died a prisoner, and his grandson Enzio fell into Bolognese hands.

Even his friend Peter of Vinea, chancellor of the Sicilian empire and creator of the new law book, betrayed him; his doctor tried to poison him. In Germany only the free imperial towns and some small knights remained with him. Soon after his army had suffered a heavy defeat near Parma, he caught malaria and died, taking refuge in one of his fortresses at Florentino, on 13th December 1250; he died in the arms of his son Manfred.

Legend transferred him—the grandson of Barbarossa—to the Kyffhauser mountain. Now that he was dead he became a legendary figure to the Germans. His tomb, however, was in Palermo Cathedral, which he founded.

The Pope now saw himself within reach of the throne of the Western Empire. Supremacy was within his grasp. He cursed the Emperor's sons, Conrad IV and Manfred, summoned Charles of Anjou's French army to Naples, and led them to destroy the Ghibellines in Italy.

The Hohenstaufens were finished. In 1268 the last of their heroes, Konradin of Swabia, with neither title nor crown, led a hopeless campaign to try to win back the Norman kingdom in Italy. The French and Italians defeated him near Tagliacozzo, captured the sixteen-year-old hero, and beheaded him in the market place of Naples.

Germany lapsed into the Interregnum (1256–1273), that "terrible time without an emperor". All the princes were fighting each other, seeking power for their own houses, as well as territory, rights, and, of course, the now vacant "regalia" (imperial rights). A few spurious kings presented themselves, for example, William of Holland, Richard of Cornwall and Alfonso X of Castile, but they never even came to Germany, and disappeared again into the oblivion of history. There was no sovereign, no imperial authority, and no law other than that of the sword.

Only the towns, surrounded by their walls, afforded protection to the ordinary people. These began to form civil leagues, to defend themselves against the princes' arbitrary actions, and against the unruly counts and knights.

With the advent of a money-based society, the social positions which had developed from feudal dues, from the work of the increasingly exploited peasants, and from participation in Crusades and in the Italian campaign, had all been swept aside; knights had become robber-knights, while troubadours and crusaders had become highwaymen. The people took the law into their own hands and formed secret organizations, such as the vehmic courts; the merchants employed travelling servants to escort their goods convoys; the townsmen kept watch on their ramparts.

Citizens' councils struggled desperately against the high tolls imposed by the land-owners; within the towns the guilds fought the patricians and nobles for the right to take part in local government.

It was a time of great disorder, a time when everyone longed for an emperor and a more ordered existence. But the days of Hohenstaufen power and prosperity were gone for ever.

King Conradin with falcons. Miniature from the Maness manuscript, about 1300.

4 No Glory and no Center

During the reign of the Hohenstaufens the European nations had turned fervently to religion, which came to permeate their entire lives. The idea of a "Christian Western Empire" had been born, to be united under *one* Church and under the spiritual supremacy of the Pope. Peasants, burghers and knights had all dreamed of an Empire ruled over by *one* Emperor as protector and judge. The German nation, which had always, both geographically and politically, been nothing more than a phantom, had had an *ideal* center in the Church and Empire.

This preoccupation with ideas gave birth, in the 13th century, to the poetry and works of Walther von der Vogelweide, Wolfram von Eschenbach, Hartmann von Aue, and to the national epic of the *Nibelungenlied*; the new "Gothic" style of architecture, which had come over from France, was brought from the peasants' cottages to the towns of Germany; the cathedrals of Cologne, Strasburg, Ulm, Freiburg and Vienna were begun, and leapt up to Heaven like towering walls of flame. Germany was gripped by scholasticism and mysticism, the greatest intellectual and spiritual advances in western culture; the sciences taken over from the Arabs and Greeks were mingled with the mystique of religion.

This era evolved out of the struggle between the two great powers, between Pope and Emperor; the realm without an Emperor lapsed into unrestrained chaos; the papacy, which had robbed itself of its greatest protector, was at the mercy of national interests and local rulers, and was transferred to distant Avignon, where it came under the severe discipline of the French. The dream of the Middle Ages slowly gave way to a sober awakening into the battle-ridden world of Realism.

The 14th century was a time of weakness and disruption. The stars which had shone over the unity of life and belief during the Middle Ages, faded at the dawn of the new era. The old forces of the papacy, sovereignty and knighthood now succumbed to new powers which were irresistibly approaching: the humanism of the intellectuals, the proud bourgeoisie of the towns, the true egoism of the princes, the awakening nationalist feeling among the surrounding nations, and the change in military technology.

"First law" brought the breakdown of German law and order to such a point, that a "college" of the seven

39

Document bearing the seals of King Rodolph I of Habsburg.

tion to his adversary in Bohemia. Rudolf banished Ottokar from the Empire, claimed the conquered lands of Austria, Styria, Carinthia and Krain for the empire, and invested his sons Albrecht and Rudolf with them; a few years later he also let them have the Tyrol. King Ottokar was defeated and killed on the battlefield at Marchfeld. Rudolf hurriedly married his own daughter to the heir of Bohemia, so as to establish future rights of succession. Meanwhile, the German princes realised that they had elected a man of their own type, that is, a realist, who understood perfectly that a ruler was only as strong as his own family possessions.

Rudolf of Habsburg was suddenly no longer a king or an emperor with a halo; no mystical majesty sur-

most powerful princes was formed: they were the Archbishops of Cologne, Trier and Mainz, the Count of the Rhein Palatinate, the Duke of Saxony, the Margrave of Brandenburg and the King of Bohemia. These rulers were intent on "liberty", and wanted to choose a king or emperor who would not interfere with, or threaten, their own power. The king should be just strong enough to control the common people, the knights and the less-powerful counts. The men of the Church wanted a man who was pious and dedicated to religion.

The man who fulfilled all these requirements was Count Rudolf of Habsburg, who held lands in Switzerland and Alsace, but was not *too* powerful. His piety could not be disputed. In 1273 the princes elected him king at Frankfurt; they crowned him at Aachen, and only King Ottokar of Bohemia refused to acknowledge him as his superior. He was himself a king, and during the Interregnum had managed to amass a kingdom stretching from the Ore Mountains, across Bohemia to Carinthia, and as far as the Adriatic.

Rudolf of Habsburg first established order by hanging a few robber-barons and having their castles demolished; then he turned his atten-

40

Below: panoramic view of a typical town in the Middle Ages; here, Aix-la-Chapelle.

rounded him. His crown had lost its glory, and was worth only the value of its gold. The succession of German kings and "Roman Emperors" who followed Rudolf of Habsburg had much in common: they all strove to strengthen their family's position, they acted in their own interests, they lacked great ideas, and all occupied a wretched position, caught between the princes, Church politics and outside enemies; all this continued until Frederick III (1438), when the Austro-Habsburg line established a form of hereditary succession. Land-grabbing, the lust for power, money and the exploitation of others, most particularly the peasants and the knights, were highly characteristic of this period. The intellectual and spiritual atmosphere of the times changed quickly in the 14th century.

After the Great Plague of 1348, the fanaticism of the scourgers and the persecution of Jews, humanity as a whole, including the deeply-religious German nation, turned their gaze away from the cathedral altars, left the towers of these great cathedrals staring uncompleted at Heaven, and turned to the realities of this world. The doors were slowly opening on a new world concerned with this life, and reviving the spirit of Humanism.

The Great Plague of 1348 represented a turning-point of history, when the "Black Death", brought from the east, killed, according to Guy de Chauliac's statistics, 48 million of Europe's estimated population of 100 million. In Lübeck, for example, the plague is said to have killed 90,000 of the 100,000 inhabitants; in Vienna, between 500 and 700 died each day, and in Nuremberg the population sank from 80,000 to 20,000; many Italian towns lost three-quarters of their population. Everywhere the doctors went through the streets wearing facemasks and pointed hats and carrying their smoke bottles; mass graves were dug and bodies were burned. Evil rumors spread, saying that the Jews had poisoned the wells, that their magic arts and misdeeds were to blame for the pestilence, and so a terrible new wave of persecution flared up around the Rhine, the Danube and in Lower Germany.

Hosts of flagellants travelled the highways and tried to avoid God's Judgment by indulging in asceticism, penance and self-inflicted torment.

An emperor investing a lord and handing him the banner which is the symbol of his new fief. The lower picture shows a procession of princes, counts and lords bearing the "bannieri," the distinctive emblems of their houses.

Witches, heretics and strangers were hunted; madness was rife.

Others escaped from the Black Death and other dangers, and delivered themselves up to the full life, held wild orgies, indulged in free love and revelled in intemperance and hedonism. Even in the Church, the so-called protector of morals and religion, the pioneer of social freedom and justice, the most extreme disparities were evident. The Franciscans, those mendicant friars, advocated the ancient Christian virtues of poverty and equality; at the same time in Avignon, the exiled popes and Church princes amassed money in their coffers.

In 1316, when Emperor Ludwig the Bavarian led a campaign against the rich Pope John XXII, the Emperor had a war fund of 1800 silver pennies, whilst the Pope had 22 million gold ducats.

During the Plague, more than 100,000 Franciscan monks and nuns died caring for the sick; in the archbishops' palaces and the princely abbeys there were noisy feasts, the high clergy went hunting with their ladies, mercilessly collected their tithes, which the peasants were forced to yield, and which burghers had to pay for every negotiation with the priests.

With the spread of humanism and the founding of more new universities (Prague, about 1348; Vienna, 1365; Heidelberg, 1366; Cologne, 1388; Erfurt, 1392), the Latin and Greek languages and cultures spread like shadows over the German folk culture. In place of the traditional peasants' rights and the old, comprehensible German law principles, the new Latin-speaking court jurisdiction was introduced. Roman law replaced the old Germanic law; the burghers found themselves caught up in complicated court chancelleries, the peasants sank more and more into bondage and serfdom and stood helpless in the face of the learned Latin world.

The Franciscans' struggle against poverty, the universities with their philosophical discussions, and the scientific work of the humanists, all put the new prevailing social order in danger; they criticised this order, demanded complete reform, and put forward political demands.

The Church was weakened by the absence of the popes in Avignon (1309–1370), by the decay of her own organization and by the schism caused by having more than one papal throne at the same time (1378–1415), so she had to consent, at a series of councils and diets, to the reforms put forward by the university professors, princes and learned laymen for her re-organization.

Everything which had once been a stable force, now seemed distinctly shaky and unreliable.

The rulers of this new era relied solely upon money and power. Wherever they felt strong enough they tore apart the old freedom rights, the Emperor's letters of safe conduct, the deeds of imperial supremacy, such as had been established by the Hohenstaufens. The Habsburg monarchs also tried this in the 13th century, when they acquired government and jurisdiction of some Swiss territories. Three cantons around Lake Lucerne, Schwyz, Uri and Unterwalden, had, however, been granted the freedom of the Empire by the Hohenstaufens, but the Habsburgs only acknowledged these old documents for Uri. They sent in their newly-acquired army of knights from the Tyrol and Styria, so as to extend their family possessions to include Switzerland. The three cantons swore a *Rütli* oath and resisted

the princes' invasion with their old peasant forms of defense. In a narrow mountain pass near Morgarten, in 1315, the mountain peasants ambushed the proud knights, who suffered a great defeat. It was proved for the first time that mobile foot-soldiers armed only with lances, given the right territory, could overcome armored knights on their heavy horses. The advent of the crossbow had forced the knights to use heavier armor and stronger horses; for bolts from the cross-bow could penetrate a light coat of mail. They now had to wear weighty iron armor, and lost their mobility because of it. This was the beginning of the end for the knightly troops, and the Swiss Lancers rose in importance.

The new confederacy then joined up with Lucerne in 1332, Zürich in 1351, Glaris and Zug in 1352 and Berne in 1353; they all made up the Confederation of the "eight ancient places". The Confederation defended their freedom in successful battles at Sempach (1386) and Näfels (1388). In the following century, all the Habsburg possessions in Switzerland were lost to this union, which increased steadily until 1513, when it represented a total of thirteen cantons.

The Swiss peasants and burghers, helped by their favorable geographical position, had shown how the people of a country thrown into disorder by its ruling upper classes, and lacking any central imperial power, could set about establishing their own rule of freedom and law.

This Empire, with its rival princes, its decadent Church, and its usually powerless Emperor, had indeed betrayed its own concepts and lost its central guiding force. Even Charles IV's Golden Bull, issued in 1356 in Metz and Nuremberg to deal with

laws governing imperial territory, could not alter the situation; this bull gave the seven elector-princes, as well as their sole right of election, a number of "regalia", formerly regal rights, and now also the highest jurisdiction, and almost complete sovereignty over their own specific areas.

In such an empire, where the princes reigned supreme and the emperor was powerless, anyone who wished to extend his possessions, take part in trade, or increase his power, had to take the law into his own hands. It was for this reason that the co-operative unions and guilds developed more and more: anyone who stood alone in this sort of world was lost. The newly-rich imperial towns, whose interests always conflicted with those of the princes, had also realised this fact.

In 1376, led by the city of Ulm, 14 Swabian towns joined together to form the Swabian Town League; the Rhine towns followed suit. The Emperor Charles, and, later, King Wenceslas, tried in vain to outlaw these leagues; the Golden Bull strictly forbade such unions, but to no effect; Count Eberhard of Württemberg failed to suppress them. When the Archbishop of Salzburg, an ally of the towns, was taken prisoner by the Duke of Bavaria, there was a great war of the towns (1388–89), which was finally quelled with great difficulty by the king. Even the imperial knights formed an alliance, the League of St. George and St. William.

In the north, however, the "Hanse", meaning "league", or "guild" developed. In 1241 Hamburg and Lübeck had already formed such an alliance in order to protect their foreign and German trade. In 1367 the Hanseatic towns joined the Cologne Confederation. There were three main parts to this, with regional headquarters in Lübeck, Cologne and Brunswick; the German Hanse had head offices in Bruges, Bergen, London and Novgorod. Soon a hundred coastal and inland towns joined the league. They acted according to the ideals of the Golden Bull: "A realm which is not united within itself, will finally become a wilderness." Lübeck was at the head of the Hanse, and had long controlled sea trade along the Baltic and west coasts. In 1361 the Danish king, Waldemar Atterdag, began a naval war against Lübeck. When, in 1362, he conquered Wisby, a Hanseatic town on the island of Gottland, he was met by the whole united forces of the Hanseatic towns, and defeated so convincingly that he even lost his own land. But in 1397 a turning point was reached. The whole of Scandinavia, Denmark, Sweden and Norway, joined the Kalmar Union. Bands of pirates, known as the *"Vitalienbrüder"* were making the

Baltic and North Sea unsafe. The English were beginning to take their trade and sea travel into their own hands, and in the Low Countries Italian merchants were interfering with German trade. The national forces of the countries where the German Hanse had its offices, markets and ports, were beginning to stir. The Hanse had no support whatever in any one state. The Empire was dragging its sickness, its too-powerful princes, its disunity, provincialism, religious decay and imperial weakness towards a new century, which would see the awakening of nations and states surrounding the Empire. Thus the ruin of the Hanseatic towns began. The northern seas of the Germans—from Lake Ladoga, across the Norwegian mountains, as far as the London docks—fell into the hands of the newly-emerged surrounding national states.

A similar fate awaited another union, which had developed its own

colonial territory, apart from the Emperor and Empire. Since the appearance of the crusading order of Teutonic Knights in East Prussia, who had built their Marienburg Castle at Danzig, and, together with fighting Friars of the *"Schwertbrüderorden"*, had converted Prussians, Kaschubs, Lithuanians, Poles and Estonians, in bloody battles, to Christianity and German culture, a whole century had passed. Under the rule of the Grand Master, Winrich von Kniprode, came the golden age of chivalric lords (1351–1382). When, however, this order lost its crusading ideals, after its mission of colonization, it, too, sank, wallowing in the fruits of what it had achieved, and fell into dispute with the resident noble and bourgeois forces, who were demanding the right to take part in and contribute to their government. Even the Hanse turned against the chivalric order, when it began to get involved in trading activities, and offer some form of competition.

A harbor scene during the heyday of the Teutonic Hansa: shipowners and merchants meeting at the customs office. The Customary of the town of Hamburg, 1497.

Meanwhile the Poles and Lithuanians had united to form a new force.

The struggle began when the Poles demanded a free passage to the sea. There was no realm that would aid the order of knights, battling as they were far away in the east. So the whole burden of the war rested with the few knights, led by Grand Master Ulrich von Jungingen, who were defeated in the year 1410 near Tannenberg.

However, even by this time, the knights had not learned their lesson. They slaughtered themselves in internal struggles, fell into new disputes with the towns and native nobility, who eventually formed a conspiracy against them, and forced them to succumb to the Treaty of Thorn in 1466. West Prussia was yielded to Poland, East Prussia became a Polish fief. The Grand Master transferred his seat from Marienburg to Königsberg.

The last Grand Master was Albrecht of Hohenzollern, who supported Luther's teachings during the

Reformation, founded a dynasty, and with the permission of the weak Polish King Sigismund, founded a hereditary principality. Kurland became a Polish fief, Livonia, Estonia and Lithuania were made over to Poland and Sweden. The dream of German colonization of the east was over, yet the Empire had scarcely noticed it and had allowed many valuable opportunities to slip away, while doing nothing to remedy the situation. The Empire and Emperor were meanwhile getting themselves more and more involved in the question of the lamentable condition of the Church and the clergy. The popes had, however, returned from the decadent Avignon court to Rome, but some members of the body of cardinals, having taken a liking to the free life of the court in Avignon, had stayed on there for a second election, so that there were now two popes in the western world, continually condemning and excommunicating each other. The Diet of Pisa had tried in vain to mend the rift: the result had simply been the election of a third Pope. Everywhere the archbishops, bishops and abbots, the canons, prelates and legates were living in the style of worldly princes; many monasteries were following this example, whilst the people were incited, by the sale of indulgences and salvation tokens, against the immorality of the priesthood. From England came the writings of Wycliffe, a humanist from Oxford, who used fiery language to condemn the papacy, calling it an invention of the devil, called the Pope an anti-Christ and spoke out against the monastic life, celibacy and indulgences. He even wanted to abolish auricular confession and Communion.

Professor John Huss of the University of Prague further expounded these heresies, and vehemently de-

Johannes Gutenberg (1400–1468) discovered printing with mobile embossed lettering. Print made in 1584.

nounced the inordinate wealth and the temporal power of Church leaders, the abuses of the monastic life and the sale of indulgences. The Czech students became his followers, whilst the German students remained faithful to the old Church. There were protests, and finally the Germans left Prague and founded the new university of Leipzig (1409).

In order to put an end to all this unrest by introducing reforms, the Pope, at Emperor Sigismund's request, called the Council of Constance in 1414. More than 50,000 people, consisting of princes, clergy, academics, humanists and burghers arrived in this small town on Lake Constance. Significantly, at the head of the reform party was the chancellor of Paris university, Gerson. The Council itself was the occasion for great festivals and pageants, such as the investiture of the Nuremberg count, Frederick of Hohenzollern, with the Marches of Brandenburg. John Huss was then

summoned to Constance, given a letter of safe conduct and an imperial guarantee, so that he could recant his heretical doctrines. When Huss refused to do this, the council condemned him to death at the stake (1415). Apart from this, the presumptuous assembly achieved nothing but the deposition of three popes and the election of a fourth. The Emperor's betrayal of John Huss, and the failure of the Council to achieve any decisive results, gave rise to the Hussite rebellion in Bohemia. The Czechs once more discovered their national feeling, and declared that they had had enough of German disorder and confusion. Johann Ziska led his army of peasants, freemen, burghers and laborers against the feudal knights. Cornered outside Wagenburgen, the

people's army destroyed all the envoys sent from the rulers' army, then
broke out in plundering masses
throughout the Palatinate and Franconia, burning down monasteries,
towns and castles as they went. Eventually they burned and murdered their
way through Saxony, Thuringia,
Brandenburg, Silesia and Austria. It
was not until the rebels split up into
religious sects that they could be overcome. At last, in 1436, Sigismund,
who had by now been crowned Emperor in Rome, was able to stop their
entry into Prague. He died one year
later. The Councils of Basle
(1431–1449), Ferrara and Florence,
as far as Church reform was concerned, all proved to be as ineffective
as the previous ones. At Ferrara and
Florence there were deputations from
the oppressed Greeks, and finally the
last Byzantine Emperor appeared in
person to beg the Emperor, Empire
and the whole of the Western World
for help for Constantinople, which
was surrounded by Turks and struggling to save the last remnants of the
Eastern Roman Empire.

However, the Empire, by this time
emptied of its ideas, was no longer capable of fulfilling this Christian duty.
Its people stood by as Europe's out-
post on the Bosphorus fell into the
hands of an Asiatic power (1453).

In Germany, another Habsburg
king was at last elected, and later
crowned Roman Emperor—Frederick III (1440–1493). The chronicles
refer to him as "the night-cap of the
German Empire". He was so poor,
especially compared to towns such as
Venice, whose yearly income from
taxes amounted to 20 million gold ducats, that he was held prisoner by certain towns for failing to pay his bills,
and in Bologna had to spend whole

days trading titles of count and prince for cash. He was powerless to intervene in the numerous civil wars which were taking place in Germany, such as the Nuremberg feuds, the Soester campaign, the Thuringian-Saxon civil war, or the battles raging on the western border between France, Burgundy, the Swiss and Lorraine; he was equally powerless to do anything about the decline of the East Prussian Order of Teutonic Knights and the distress of the Hanseatic towns. He could not eben retain his own inherited Austrian lands, when these were occupied by the Bohemian king.

Meanwhile the new Burgundian Empire had established itself along the western borders of the German Empire, after a struggle with the French king, and as a result of the Hundred Years' War against England, which had just ended. As in Carolingian times, Lorraine had emerged again in its own right. With its flourishing provinces of Flanders, Brabant, Burgundy, Lorraine and certain French areas, this great new state was significant, powerful and rich. Here was the last blossoming of the chivalric age; the arts, sculpture, architecture, fashion, great festivities and chivalrous life reached the peak of their medieval development. Yet it was a dream state with open borders, disconnected in places, filled with the feudal spirit of its dukes, but unsupported by the will or enthusiasm of its burghers, peasants and native tribes. Charles the Bold set out with a magnificent army of nobles to force the resisting confederates into submission to his empire. Near Murten he lost his cavalry, near Granson his artillery, and near Nancy his life (1477). His heir was a beautiful eighteen-year-old girl called Mary, whom both the King of France and the German Emperor's son sought to marry. The French king was over fifty, a hunch-back with a jealous nature; Maximilian, Emperor Frederick's son, was nineteen and carried home all the prizes at the Trier Tournament. He was the last of the "knight-kings".

Mary married Maximilian, so that the house of Habsburg acquired the

49

Jakob Fugger and his secretary Matthäus Schwarz. At the Fugger bank in Augsburg, business went hand in hand with the indulgence market. The Fuggers handled this business for the Vatican on a commission basis.

lion's share of the Burgundian Empire. Mary died young as a result of a riding accident. but she gave Maximilian a son, Philip the Handsome, who married Isabel, the only daughter of Ferdinand of Aragon and Isabel of Castile, and thus the heiress to the Spanish kingdom. The grandson of Emperor Maximilian, Charles V, was to inherit not only the Burgundian empire with Flanders and the Low Countries, the crown of the Empire along with the Austrian inheritance, but also Milan and the imperial possessions in Italy and Spain; thus he was to inherit Upper and Lower Italy and the colonies; it was to be "the empire on which the sun never sets".

For the first time the saying was heard: "Let others wage wars; you, happy Austria, make marriages". Maximilian I (1493–1519), by his marriage, gave the Empire its last, world-wide chance.

Everything else about the handsome Maximilian, whose portrait and prayer-book we know from Dürer's picture, was typical of the Habsburgs: he was an Emperor without a halo. He was most concerned for his family possessions, looked after Austria, and only bothered with the Empire as a secondary consideration. He abolished feudal rights and decreed an "eternal peace"; he established the *Reichskammergericht* as the final jurisdiction for the settlement of future disputes between rival powers – but then immediately devalued it by establishing an upper jurisdiction at the *Reichshofrat* in Vienna. In order to put an end to imperial money troubles, he ordered the first imperial taxes to be collected; these were known as the *"Allgemeiner Pfennig"* (universal penny), and in order to facilitate their collection, he divided the realm into ten districts. Unfortunately

for him, however, most of the Germans would not pay the penny. They put their money into the poor-boxes, donated for monasteries, churches and St. Peter, and paid dearly for indulgences. And yet Maximilian stood at the entrance to a new era. The world was changing rapidly, and Germany and the Empire were no exception. The first part of the Middle Ages was finished by 1517, the second part did not really end until four hundred years later, in 1917. But this second part was at the same time a prelude to modern times.

The arts, as the record-keepers of history, had shown numerous changes. The Heaven-bound flames of the Gothic spirit had changed to the horizontal architecture of Antiquity, that is, to the Renaissance. Ever since Giotto, painting had sought to represent outward reality rather than inner truth; the period of "late-Gothic realism" (with Van Eyck, Memmling and Schongauer) brought horizontal lines, nature, animals and plants, and individual characteristics were depicted in the faces painted. The learned study of scholasticism gave way to philological, historical and scientific studies. The fame of German humanists such as Erasmus of Rotterdam, Conrad Celtis, Pirkheimer, Peutinger, Reuchlin and Ulrich von Hutten shone brightly throughout Europe.

Holbein, Dürer, Baldung Grien, Altdorfer and Lukas Cranach now appeared.

The feeling of a re-birth of the spirit of Antiquity, known as the Renaissance, spread from Italy and mingled with the new German national spirit.

The new world which was awakening rested on four pillars: four evangelists of a religion which was turning its face to this world created a change of consciousness. Around

*Below: Charles V, in 1548, by Titian.
Opposite page: Charles V and Pope
Clement VII at the crowning of the
Emperor in Bologna (print by
Nicolas Hogennerg)*

1450 John Gutenberg invented the art of printing in Mainz, and thereby created the technical possibility for the mass circulation of books, pamphlets, and newspapers. Propaganda, as well as knowledge, could now be spread. Both education and politics could benefit from this "black art" which spread like a forest fire from Mainz across Germany and the whole of Europe. In 1492 Christopher Columbus sailed to America, which he thought was part of the East Indies; he finally proved by his voyage what Martin Behaim from Nuremberg had claimed when he built his first globe, and what the humanists maintained: that the earth was spherical, and not flat, as the Church had taught. If, however, the world was not flat, with the Redeemer's grave in the centre, and the pope as His earthly administrator, but was spherical, then *one* belief alone could not be correct, and *one* bishop in Rome could not remain as God's sole representative on earth.

The German canon, Nicolas Kopernikus, from Thorn, finally taught his theory that the planets rotate around the sun, and that the Earth was a grain of dust somewhere on the edge of one of the solar systems. This cut to the heart of medieval-Christian teachings: with this new theory it became unlikely that Man was the reason for the Creation and the sole object of redemption.

It was out of this atmosphere that the fourth evangelist emerged, shouting, into the modern age Martin Luther, a monk and professor from Wittenberg. It was he who gave the first push to the tottering structure of the Church; he set the Gospels above the organised Church, and gave the oppressed people his revolutionary theses on "the freedom of the Christian being".

52

5 From Empire to Patchwork Quilt

Around the turn of the 15th–16th centuries, most German towns were involved in the struggle for participation, and the guilds were fighting for their part in civic government. As trade, crafts and many types of art were blossoming, the towns, with their walls and moats, their towers and archways, reflected a rich, rural culture. There was a distinct increase in the cost of oriental goods such as spices, dyes, sugar and precious metals, since the Turks and Arabs had recently been blockading the eastern Mediterranean. For the same reason there was an increasing shortage of money, for money consisted almost exclusively of coins, and Europe had hardly any source of precious metals.

The knights were all in an even worse position. The big landowners were trying to press them into ever greater dependence, and their sources of income from the Italian campaigns and crusades had dried up. What remained was the exploitation of the few villages and their peasant populations who lived in serfdom under the control of a castle. Thus the knighthood suffered from dwindling capital, lack of cash, dependence on the peasants living in the shadow of a castle or monastery, from bondage and drudgery, and the arbitrary, even barbaric punishments meted out during a time when rights and freedom had disappeared as never before.

The condition of the Church was hardly favorable; Rome was occupied by pompous, ostentatious popes, obsessed with money, power and luxurious living; archbishops, bishops and abbots could scarcely be distinguished from worldly princes in their way of life, morals and open enjoyment of worldly pleasures. Many monasteries were hotbeds of vice; gluttony, debauchery and fornication

spread freely through the canons' and prelates' houses. The saddest fact of all was that the German people, still on the whole deeply religious, were increasingly at the mercy of the Church's sales of indulgences, trade in religious relics and unscrupulous money dealings. Pope Leo X had begun, not only to make his Roman court the most splendid in Europe, but also to build up St. Peter's as the most powerful church in the world. He needed enormous sums of money for these projects, and obtained these sums by selling pieces of paper to the Germans, granting them the remission of earthly sins, and by selling the remains of martyrs' bodies from the catacombs. The chief representative for these religious articles in Germany was archbishop Albrecht of Brandenburg, who owned Mainz, Magdeburg

and Halberstadt. In the sale of indulgences the primate worked together with James Fugger's merchant banking house. His agents filled the German districts with market-place sales-talk. One of the most successful and, of course, least scrupulous of the travelling indulgence-salesmen was a Dominican monk called Tetzel.

There were other types of travellers wandering through the lands: vagrants, travelling students, fallen priests, fanatical preachers of penitence, rabble-rousers, most of whom shouted loudly for reform and demanded a change in society. On 31st October 1517 the Augustinian monk, Professor Martin Luther, nailed his famous 95 theses on the reform of the Church to the door of the church in Wittenberg; in this same church 17,443 pieces of holy relics were on

display. The church was the proud possession of the pious Elector Frederick of Saxony, and yielded him the appropriate amount of interest; those who knelt and prayed in this church gained—according to the calculations of Luther's friend, the humanist Spalatin—127,799 years' and 116 days' indulgence each time. Luther had been to Rome in 1511, and Tetzel had preached in his district: he had had enough of this sort of piety and formed his thoughts of reform as a professor and theologian; by publishing his theses he challenged the world to discuss his revolutionary principles.

Luther had only envisaged a literary feud, foreseen a series of pamphlets about his theses, and learned disputations. But the people took notice; they cheered and encouraged the monk and professor, who nevertheless reminded them humbly of their duty to obey the Pope and Church (1519). It was only when the fanatical professor from Ingolstadt, Dr. Eck, incited Luther, and Luther decided to take up some of John Huss's doctrines, that the situation became more threatening. Other humanists now began to side with Luther, for example the young Philip Melanchthon,

but Luther's opponents managed to get him excommunicated. When, on 30th December 1520, he publicly burned the papal bull and the Church law book in front of the *Elstertor* in Wittenberg, he broke finally with the Church.

As the Lutheran rebellion spread like a whirlwind through the towns, universities and districts, the whole issue assumed a political significance. In 1521, the papal legate, after a journey to parliament, reported back to Rome that he had scarcely met any remaining faithful followers of the Roman Church in Germany.

Below, right: the traditional order under threat: peasants, artisans and landsknechts (footsoldiers) revolt against the nobility and the clergy.

Meanwhile, Charles V of the Netherlands, Emperor designate, had been crowned in Aachen; he was financed by the houses of Fugger and Welser, and travelled to the parliament in Worms. He summoned Martin Luther before him.

In the presence of princes, high clergy, knights and burghers, the little monk boldly maintained his reform thesis, which he supported with proof from the Gospels. He refused to recant and to promise obedience, and won the Germans' hearts with his simple appearance and his courage. The Emperor outlawed him as a heretic, but Luther's sovereign made sure that he was brought safely back to his home. Disguised as "Junker Jörg" he lived for half a year at the Wartburg castle. Here he began to translate the Holy Scriptures into German. Using the High German of the Saxon chancelleries, he established a generally-accepted form of written language for the German nation.

While Luther was living in the Wartburg, the general decay of the Church's power in Germany increased, powerful emotion gripped the hearts of the people, and the suppressed hatred of the clergy broke loose. Monks ran away from the monasteries, the clergy took wives, the people destroyed relics, sculptures, altars and holy vestments. An enthusiast named Karlstadt gave the chalice to the laymen and spoke out against images and ceremony; in Zwickau simple laborers became baptizers of men. All this developed into pillage and riots against the men of the Church.

Luther then stepped in, quietened the uproar, and showed, by carefully constructing a model of an evangelical parish, how he envisaged and desired the regeneration of the Church to be.

call for "evangelical freedom". Later movements, such as that of Thomas Münzer in Thuringia developed almost communist tendencies.

Throughout the whole realm, with the exception of Bavaria, where bondage and serfdom had never existed, armed masses emerged. Especially around Lake Constance, in the Allgäu and Swabia, in Thuringia, the Rhine-Moselle area, the Tyrol and Upper Austria, in all these lands with many small monasteries and knightly overlords, where exploitation of the peasants had been particularly merciless, armies of enraged peasants attacked monasteries, castles and small towns. The peasants even chose a banner for themselves—it was to be black, red and gold; to the imperial colors of black and gold had been added the red of liberty. For these people, who had long been oppressed, exploited and tormented, were not looking for anarchy: they wanted an empire of justice with a strong Emperor at its head. They still cherished in their hearts the dream of Hohenstaufen days, when the Emperor had been the champion of the weak and the protector of their rights. Wendel Hippler, the clerk of the peasant band, was working in Heilbronn on a new imperial constitution, in which the possessions of clerical rulers would be secularised, the princes would be divested of their power, and an empire of free peasants, burghers and knights would be ruled over by a people's Emperor.

Their "Twelve Articles", which were proclaimed at Memmingen, demanded the abolition of serfdom and bondage, the placing of severe restrictions on the death levies, the free election of priests, and the re-establishment of all their old rights. The rebellion was taking on social-revolu-

The basis of the church service was to be preaching and song, the Bible was to be the sole foundation for the doctrine. He believed in a mature Christian being, answerable only to his conscience, and he advised the state and society as a whole to reform and change itself. In his pamphlets he called upon the councils of all German towns to establish schools, he reminded the princely overlords of the need for justice, and announced to the people the "Liberty of the Christian man".

Such notions fell like sparks onto the gunpowder of the times. Around the central Rhine area and in the Palatinate the oppressed imperial knights, led by Luther's friend, Franz von Sickingen, had already rebelled against the princes (1522–23). They were defeated in their medieval castles by the cannons of the rulers. Sickingen was killed and the great humanist, Ulrich von Hutten, mortally wounded, had to flee as an outlaw into the free country of Switzerland. But in the meantime a more dangerous and sinister uprising was being prepared; the Peasants' War of 1524–25 broke out.

There had already been some local uprisings of the tormented peasants, who were always denied their rights by all and sundry; peasant leagues had secretly been formed, such as the *"Bundschuh"* in the Rhine area, and the *"Arme Konrad"* in Swabia. Two movements clashed with each other: the peasants were fighting for the old Germanic *Volksrecht* to be re-introduced, and they took up Luther's

56

Facing: Protestant princes. Below, right: on the scales of justice the peasant, bound hand and foot, weighs more than his master.

tionary tendencies. Unfortunately, things turned out differently in reality: the uncontrolled peasant mobs went on a wild rampage, looting, torturing and raping as they went, burning castles and monasteries. Their campaigns, despite the sound leadership of experienced warrior-knights such as Florian Geyer and Götz von Berlichingen, lacked discipline and strategy. Because of their terrifying excesses they soon lost the sympathy of their potential confederates in the towns and the guilds. The whole of feudal society turned against them, and even Martin Luther issued a pamphlet "against the thieving and murderous peasants". The professor had not suspected what effects his class-room theories could have upon the people.

Emperor Charles, with the aid of an army of foot-soldiers, had just defeated and captured his enemy, Francis I of France, in the vineyards of Pavia (February 1525). Now he sent the troops of George von Frundsberg to the aid of the Swabian federation. The peasant armies soon succumbed to the troops and the armored nobility. The overlords then held terrible penal courts. They responded to this unsuccessful bid for freedom with torture, mass executions, year-long pursuits of rebels and even worse suppression of the peasant population. It was at this time that the peasant became society's beast of burden, the stupid "country bumpkin", at the complete mercy of his overlord. The idea of a German national spirit, and the timid attempt at democracy, were put off for a long time to come: a state involving the complete subjection of the people was established in the Empire. Luther wrote yet another controversial pamphlet—"against the raging, senseless tyrants, who have

not had their fill of blood, even after the battle''.

However, the idea of the Reformation had by this time been taken completely out of the reformer's hands. It had become a matter of politics in the hands of the princes, a matter of business in the hands of the burghers. Many landowners, for example, those in Saxony, Brandenburg and Hesse, changed over to the side of the Evangelists; princes of the Church joined Luther's party so that they could marry and then bequeath their fiefs to their heirs—for example, Albrecht of Brandenburg now became a duke of East Prussia. Many of the Church and monastery estates were sold into the hands of the burghers, so that they too came to believe strongly in the evangelical cause, otherwise they would have to give back all the lands they had gained in this way.

In the ensuing spread of rebellion against the papacy and the Roman Church, the dividing line which now developed between the Protestant and Catholic areas roughly followed the geographical pattern which had formerly separated the region influenced by the Mediterranean and Rome from the freer area of Germania: that is, a line stretching from the Rhine to the Main, across the *limes* as far as the Danube. The area which, a thousand years before, had looked to Caesar and the Roman Empire, remained Catholic; the north and the east looked to the heathen sea and to the freedom of the Gospel and Protestantism. The Reformation quickly reached out to Denmark and Scandinavia. Then, however, it sprang up near Zurich with Ulrich Zwingli, then later (in 1536) in Geneva with Calvin, spread from there to France, the Netherlands and Scotland.

The ideological frontier ran straight through the center of Germany. The Emperor now had a new problem added to all his others—that of how to overcome this rift. Up until this time the Catholic religion had been the one thing which had united the many different tribes and races of the western world; it had bound together the realm which Charles V was to rule over. If he was to hold onto his empire he had to put himself on the side of the popes and the Church.

Charles V's long reign (1519–1554) turned into a tragic pendulum swinging between the Protestants and the princes, between France and Turkey, between politics and popes. France, now ominously surrounded by the huge Habsburg empire in Spain, Upper Italy, Burgundy, the Netherlands and Germany, tried to break through this circle and struggled with the Emperor. She looked for her allies among the dangerously increasing eastern power of the Turks, who, in 1529 had reached almost as far as Vienna. She also gave support to the *fronde* of Protestant princes who were opposing the Emperor's campaign against his own people.

Charles V had just managed, after a series of parliaments, mainly held at Augsburg, to achieve a precarious balance between the Protestants and the Church, there was just a faint hope that he might wield a united imperial power, when the French began to wage war in Italy and in the west, the Turks advanced across the Balkans against Hungary and Vienna, even the Pope joined forces with the Emperor's enemies to protect his Church State from the encircling Habsburg power.

As soon as the Emperor, after much travelling about, had overcome his foreign enemies (with the Sack of Rome, with his triumph over the French armies, sea campaigns against the pirate-states of Algiers and Tunis, and by defending his lands against the Turks) the Protestant princes in his own empire then attacked him from behind. He was forced to accept the fact that there could be no settlement of the division in the Church through parliaments and religious discussions, so he armed himself for war against the princes who had united against

The chancellor of the Prince-Elector of Saxony reads the Confession of faith of the Protestant princes to Charles V and the Diet assembled at Augsburg (1530).

him in the *Schmalkaldischer Bund*. The Protestant commander, Maurice of Saxony, the foot-soldiers under Schärtlin von Burtenbach, and the forces of the Catholic Imperial Army all helped him to win a decisive victory over the Protestant princes. The *Schmalkaldenbund* was dissolved and even the large imperial towns submitted to the Emperor. By the spring of 1547 almost the whole of southern Germany and a large part of the north had been brought back under the Emperor's power.

In Trent, a great Church Reform Council met between 1545 and 1563. Near Mühlberg, on the Elbe, the Elector of Saxony was now defeated and taken prisoner. There only remained Philip of Hesse on the Protestant side. The Emperor seemed at last to have a hold on the Empire. In 1550 another parliament met at Augsburg to decree a new, improved order for the Empire.

Then Maurice of Saxony, who had once betrayed his own Protestant brothers for the sake of the electorate

he now held, turned traitor once more. He bartered away the free imperial towns of Toul, Metz and Verdun in a secret deal with France, and in return received "subsidies" to renew the war. He went back to the Protestant side, gave the north-German territories their freedom, and quickly made his way south. The Emperor fled from Augsburg to Innsbruck, only to be overtaken by some of the traitor's horsemen; feverish, plagued by gout, his will broken, he had to flee by night over the Brenner Pass in an

61

open carriage in the rain. The emperor "on whose empire the sun never sets", the ruler of Spain, Mexico, Peru, the Philipines, of the lands from the Iberian peninsula to Upper Italy, the Netherlands and the German empire, was now powerless.

Charles V left the difficult task of making peace to his brother Ferdinand, whom he had already named as his heir in his will. In August 1552 a religious peace treaty was signed at Passau, giving all Protestant princes religious freedom. This decision was ratified in 1555 at the Augsburg parliament: religious freedom for the peers of the realm. For their subjects the question was settled by the formula: "cuis regio, eius religio"—they

would have to follow the religion of their overlord. Meanwhile Charles V had abdicated. He resigned in Brussels before an Imperial Diet and made over the Netherlands and the Spanish part of the Habsburg inheritance to his son Philip; his brother Ferdinand was to succeed him as Emperor. The wishes of the Church were respected, in that Upper Italy and Milan were to be part of the Empire, whilst southern Italy and Sicily were to remain with the Spanish part of the inheritance. The Germans still had the problem of their discord with the princes, their subservience and the religious division. Their last great emperor had been defeated by these overwhelming circumstances and died alone and al-

most forgotten in a monastery at Saint Yuste (1558).

The world which the Emperor left behind him had undergone a radical change. The Renaissance had not only brought new styles of art and building from Italy, but also a new philosophy of life. Religion had hitherto been the focal point of interest, but now the sciences and the teachings of the universities, the burghers' realism and the often cynical opportunism of the princes had taken over. In Germany itself this change took place more slowly than in other western countries. The simple German people held faithfully to their religion. The Renaissance and Humanism belonged to the intellectuals, artists and rich

Below: Tilly's hitherto undefeated army laid siege to Magdeburg in the spring of 1631. Two months later, on May 10, the town was sacked and burned.

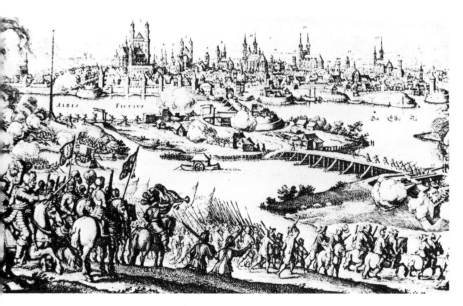

people. The peasants and laborers lived on quietly, in the oppression of their hard daily work.

Germany was still one of the most powerful and flourishing of the western countries—but unfortunately it was not a single state, but a loose cluster of individual dominions. Almost twenty-eight million people lived in the German area, whereas France had a population of about fourteen million, and England only eight million.

However, history was gradually changing and the powers of Germany and Italy were to be removed from the limelight. The importance of the north-to-south axis of Central Europe was to be removed, the significance of the Mediterranean as the central sea in the course of history was to diminish. History from now on was to revolve around the Atlantic. With the blocade of the eastern trade routes and the discovery of sea routes to America and India, along with the conquering of colonies across the ocean, the emphasis gradually moved

westwards. Germany was becoming a secondary point of interest.

When Charles V divided his inheritance, the rich Netherlands, whose population was largely of Germanic origin, was practically cut off from the Empire, thus losing for the Empire the river estuaries on the Atlantic side of the continent. The declining Hanseatic towns were in the process of losing their naval supremacy to other emerging states. In an age preoccupied with the riches of the earth, Germany had no role to play on the seas, but seemed unaware of this fact, as it was so deeply involved in its own provincial feuds and religious disputes.

The struggle between Reformation and Counter-Reformation ruled the stage at the end of the 16th century. Meanwhile the kingdoms of the west, that is, Spain, France and England, which had managed to develop as national unities, had also managed to solve their religious conflicts and unite their national and economic interests with the Church against reform. Ger-

many managed to do neither. In Paris the militant Jesuit order was founded by the Spaniard, Ignatius Loyola. The Jesuits also began to influence those in power in Germany.

Thus the Jesuit College in Munich's Neuhauserstrasse became the political center of the Counter-Reformation. Duke Maximilian of Bavaria was preaching strict Catholic politics. His colleague from the Jesuit University of Ingolstadt, who later became Emperor Ferdinand II (1619–1637), placed himself likewise in the protection of Jesuit confessors. On the opposing side the Protestants were uniting under Maximilian's Wittelsbach cousin, Elector Frederick of the Palatinate. In 1608 the Protestant princes founded their Union to protect themselves against the infringement of the Catholics in numerous conflicts over inheritance and succession rights. The Catholics then united under Duke Maximilian to form their League (1609). The dividing front line ran right through the center of Germany.

A few minor conflicts were resolved without a war, but the fuse to the gunpowder was smouldering. Yet again, just as in the days of John Huss, it was in Bohemia, and especially in its capital city of Prague, that the situation exploded. National contrasts here became mixed with the religious conflicts. The situation developed into a tumult when the Bohemians vehemently presented their petition: imperial chancellors were thrown out of the windows of Prague castle.

This event gave rise to the actual war which was to end in the destruction of the Empire. The Protestant Czechs established their own rule and called upon Frederick of the Palatinate, leader of the Union, to be their new king and to organize an army.

Johannes Kepler (1571–1630), astronomer and mathematician to Emperor Rodolph II. He discovered the laws governing the movement of the planets.

Opposite page, bottom: acquiring the confiscated property of Czech nobles, Albrecht von Wallenstein made himself an immense fortune, with which, all on his own, he raised a powerful army for use in the service of the Emperor. He was named Generalissimo.

Meanwhile, the Jesuit scholar had been made Emperor and called Ferdinand II. As he personally had neither money nor troops, he called upon his schoolfriend, Maximilian of Bavaria, for help. Maximilian had full coffers and an army of mercenaries under the strict leadership of the Dutchman Tilly; this army took up battle against the pledging of upper Austria. In 1620 the Protestants suffered an overwhelming defeat at the White Mountain near Prague; Frederick, the "Winter King" was forced to flee. He was called this because he had only reigned for a few winter months. The Union, having failed to defend the Rhineland-Palatinate, was dissolved.

However, this was not the end of the war; other Protestant princes, such as Christian of Brunswick, the Margrave of Baden and Mansfelder, rose up. Their armies were supported by those of the Netherlands and England, since these states were in conflict with the Spanish-led Counter-Reformation. When, however, Tilly's invincible Bavarian army appeared, when Mannheim and Heidelberg were taken by storm and plundered, the Catholic and Imperial cause appeared to have won the day. Duke Maximilian received his reward: in 1623 he was made Elector at the Regensburg parliament.

Almost at once, the second phase of the Great War flared up—this time in the Netherlands and in Denmark. Protestant overlords once more raised armies, this time with the help and support of King Christian IV of Denmark. Albrecht von Wallenstein, a Bohemian noble who had greatly profited by the confiscation in 1621 of Protestant territories, offered to provide the Emperor with an army, which he lured to his cause with money. Adventurers, mercenaries and uprooted peasants flocked to his support.

With the principle "the war must feed itself", Wallenstein made his way to north Germany. With Tilly he defeated all enemies, plundered the lands and conquered the Protestant areas. As his reward he was given the two duchies of Mecklenburg. Then he besieged the Hanseatic town of Stralsund; his intention was to extend the imperial power as far as the coast, and to form a German fleet. However, at Stralsund he failed to achieve his aims: the Danish king, and also Gustave Adolf of Sweden, used reinforcements to prevent the Germans creating an opening onto the sea which they considered to be their own. And so at Lübeck a hollow peace was made, which re-established the former state of affairs. In the meantime the Emperor had published his fatal Edict of Restitution (1629), which restored to the Church all its seized and secularized estates. This, of course, was highly impracticable, because in many cases almost a hundred years had elapsed and the Church possessions had changed hands a dozen times.

In 1630, at the meeting of electors at Regensburg, the Bavarians especially protested against the power and influence of Generalissimo Wallenstein. As the Emperor's helpers and

swordsmen, they now saw themselves driven into the shadows by Wallenstein, and managed to obtain his dismissal. This happened just at the time when a new, mightier enemy appeared—Gustave Adolf of Sweden had landed on German soil. He came ostensibly to the aid of other Protestants, but was secretly aiming at the creation of a great Nordic empire. He had already led campaigns in the Bal-

tic and in Poland; now he set out to gain what he could from war-torn Germany, perhaps even to become Emperor himself. The terrible Swedish phase of the war (1630–1635) began.

While Tilly was busy besieging, storming and burning down Magdeburg, the Swedes occupied northern Germany as far the Saxon frontiers. In the Battle of Breitenfeld of 1631, they used new mobile war tactics to defeat Tilly's *Landsknechte*. The end of the *lansquenet* was heralded by artillery and assault troops. The Swede marched victorious as far as Franconia, where he held court at Würzburg and formed a subsidy-alliance with France. Then he pursued Tilly to Rain on Lech, and the old champion died inside the walls of Ingolstadt, which were surrounded by Swedish troopers. The Bavarian army disbanded, Munich gave in without a battle and was plundered. War became general everywhere. Burning, plundering hordes of foreign warriors, marauders and robbers wandered through Bavaria and Swabia, the Palatinate and central Germany. In such a desperate situation only Wallenstein could help, and the Emperor gave him extraordinary authority. An army of German mercenaries, old warriors, Croats, Bohemians and Slavs was assembled. In 1632 there was a great battle at Lutzen, in which Pappenheim was killed on the imperial side, and Gustave Adolf on the Swedish side. Wallenstein seemed to rule the whole scene, but nonetheless withdrew to his native Bohemia. Perhaps he was playing with the idea of taking over as dictator in this empire which was torn apart by the sovereign princes, by party conflict and by imperial impotence. He even made deals with the Protestants, thus bringing the

wrath of the Jesuits upon him. The Bavarians and the court chancellery in Vienna were once more envious and distrustful of the mighty man. In February 1634 he was assassinated at Eger by officers who supported the Emperor.

The war continued to devastate the land from the Baltic right across to the upper Rhine. Near Nördlingen the imperial forces defeated the Swedes and Bernard of Weimar, who were fleeing westwards in search of protection from the French. At this point French politics, led by Cardinal Richelieu, entered the battle. The French war (1635–1648) followed the Swedish war. With this, the Thirty Years' War entered its cruellest phase. The Empire sank under a cloud of smoke, laid waste by murder and plundering. The eternal see-saw of the war brought inflation, and stocks of precious metals were exhausted. Peasants lived like wolves, hidden in the forests, the burghers grieved in the plundered ruins of their towns, whole areas were depopulated, and foreign

soldiers united with German blood. The princes and envoys of the rival powers finally met in Münster and Osnabruck in 1648.

The Empire, which no longer existed, was broken up into a patchwork quilt of almost fully independent sovereign states, which had only very loose links with the Crown and Empire. 378 single territories and innumerable enclaves and exclaves were recognized. The famous lawyer-teacher Pufendorf rightly denounced this agglomeration of states as "monstrous". The Emperor remained utterly powerless, the parliament, in permanent session in Regensburg, became the object of the people's scorn. Goethe said of the *Reichskammergericht* that on average it made a decision once every 35 years. The absolute power lay with the princes, those overlords and rulers of German history, who had by now exercised their "liberty" to the death. These overlords now squeezed their lands for taxes in order to keep standing armies and sumptuous courts, and to

build huge Baroque castles. In the Peace of Westfalia France took over the Austrian possessions in Alsace and Sundgau, the government of the ten Alsatian cities (with the exception of Strasbourg and Mulhouse), and also the city of Breisach on the right bank of the Rhine. The Swedes occupied part of Pomerania, Stettin, Wismar and the bishoprics of Bremen and Verden. The estuaries of the German rivers were now definitively in the hands of the Poles, Swedes and Dutch, and Wallenstein's dream of German sea-power and naval politics was truly over.

The provinces at the source and the mouth of the most German of all German rivers—the Rhine—were now also recognized as sovereign states: Switzerland and the Netherlands became independent. The loss in population was incredible: the Rhineland Palatinate, Hesse, eastern Swabia, Thuringia, Mecklenburg and Pomerania had lost between two-thirds and three-quarters of their inhabitants; in other German regions between a half and a third of the people had died. Hunger, pestilence and harsh overlords did the rest. The once-flourishing Empire was destroyed. Any sense of national consciousness had disappeared.

The Germans, especially the intellectual classes, bowed down to their victors. Where there were French they spoke French, where there were Poles, they spoke Polish, and where the Swedes were dominant they spoke Swedish. The Germans began to admire foreign fashions, foreign thought, poetry, art and ways of life. Learned men taught Latin, the princes' courts spoke French, only the dumb, foolish peasants and laborers, who worked on as before with animal-like patience, spoke the vulgar language of German.

The Peasants' War had begun by enforcing subjection upon the German masses. Now, however, the old patriarchal system of overlords and tenant-farmers, was in many areas being replaced by hereditary serfdom, which meant that the peasants were bound to the soil by a ban on their liberty of movement and by the total loss of their personal freedom. The men who now set about rebuilding the war-torn land, whose children were to renew the slaughtered nation's population, became the servants of all and the nobleman's "beast of burden".

The history of that empire which, eight hundred years earlier, had begun amid the glory of kings and emperors, was now at an end, and was dispersed among the separate ways of the miscellaneous states and princely lines.

The Golden Bull had prophesied that "an empire which is divided within itself will finally turn to desert". This point seemed to have been reached. The German nation no longer existed, the Empire was a farce, its Emperor was a poor fool and nothing more than a prince among princes.

History, in the centuries which followed, belonged more to the growing nations all around Germany—that is, to France, England, Sweden, and even to the awakening Russians.

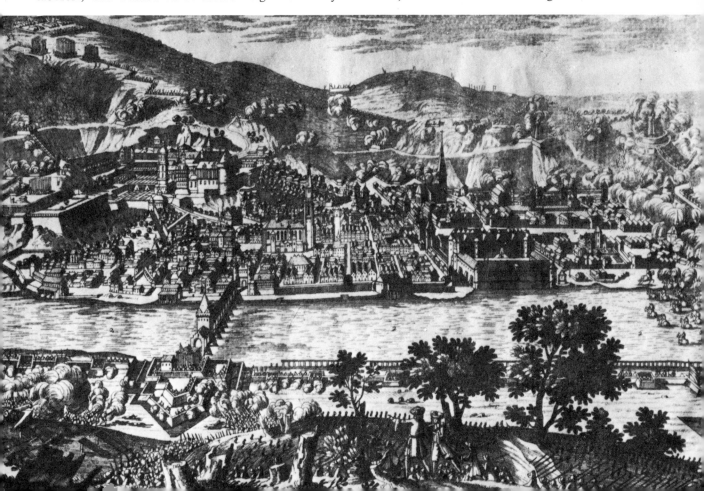

6 Swan-Song of the First Reich

After the national and cultural catastrophe of the Thirty Years' War, it was a good century-and-a-half before the German Empire was nominally dissolved. This interval—as befits any absence of order and power—was filled with new, devastating outbreaks of war, with arbitrary acts by local rulers, and with a patient, desperate struggle for survival by the ordinary people.

France's absolute ruler, the "Sun King", waged territorial wars over the western border provinces, occupied Strasbourg and took possession of Alsace and Lorraine; the French were also responsible for burning down the Palatinate and Heidelberg. In the east the massive Turkish armies overran the land as far as Vienna. In northern Germany the Brandenburg ruler was fighting the Swedes and Poles, and as soon as that struggle was over, the whole empire, from the Rhine to Bavaria, was involved in the War of the Spanish Succession, which was followed by the War of the Austrian Succession and the three great Silesian wars, which finally gave way to the revolutionary cannons and the Napoleonic campaigns. At the same time, the last traces of personal freedom disappeared. The territorial princes ruled over their towns and lands with an iron rod; monstrous amounts of taxes and labor were squeezed out of their peasants, and in Hesse and Württemberg their sons were sold as soldiers to foreign powers. These Baroque princes now had absolute power, with no participation from the lower classes, with no laws and no moral values. These overlords needed money and yet more money to finance their splendid courts, their hunts and festivals, their extravagant mistresses and corrupt officials, and to build their magnificent castles. Posterity was to

admire the wonderful palaces which were built from Würzburg to Vienna, from Munich to Hanover, at Stuttgart, Mannheim, Brühl and Berlin, and would talk of the great Baroque builders—Fischer von Erlach, Hildebrand, Dientzenhofer, Balthasar Neumann and Asam. And besides these fairy-tale castles with their lofty staircases, galleries, banqueting halls and suites of rooms, behind the magical parks with their pagodas, pavilions and fountains, around all this there arose out of the war-torn land the endless Baroque churches: there was the splendid, jubilant, colorful style of Bavaria and Austria, and the stricter, more severe style of the Protestant north. The whole land was full of architects, sculptors, painters, plasterers, and furniture-designers. It is strange how the continuing affliction and torment of the indestructible German people gave rise at this time to their greatest cultural achievements. As soon as the people had had a little time to recover from the blows of the Thirty Years' War, as soon as farms and villages had been rebuilt and the towns had been refurnished with patricians' and burghers' houses, creative talents blossomed forth to produce great artistic, cultural and scientific achievements out of the dust of political misery. Even in the Thirty Years' War, Germany had had its Johann Kepler, and now it produced the great philosopher Leibnitz. At the end of this period of war and oppression it would produce the philosophers Christian Wolff, Immanuel Kant and Fichte, along with their pupils, Hegel and Schelling. The Great War had given birth to a writer like Grimmelshausen; the ensuing decay produced a critic such as Martin Opitz. Out of these times of the greatest national impotence evolved the most

glorious age of writers: from Gellert to Klopstock, from Lessing, through Winckelmann and Wieland to Herder and Jean Paul, until the peak of poetic achievement was reached with Goethe and Schiller. Germany experienced its Classical period at the court of Weimar. The same age, which produced the obsequious "Spiessbürger" and the work-worn estate serf, the slave who was sold according to the size of his body, and the arrogant, strutting cavalier with his wigs, knee-hose and frock-coat, this age also gave birth to genius: Bach, Handel, Gluck, Haydn and Mozart emerged, and the whole epoch was crowned with the music of Ludwig von Beethoven. For the Western World, with Germany as its center, had its final fling of style just as the Baroque period was fluttering into the Rococo, and took refuge in the music of the operas, symphonies, fugues, cantatas, passions and concertos.

Germany's western neighbors, who had in the meantime turned towards the outside world with its oceans and distant continents, now looked apprehensively, yet admiringly on the politically self-destructive German nation, and recognised the stirring of genius. Half in admiration, half in scorn, they called the Germans "the nation of poets and thinkers". The Russians said that God had created man, but the Germans had created the ape. The surrounding countries began to regard this eternal turmoil with suspicion: they knew that for the moment it was harmless, because of its internal conflicts, but they also knew that it was capable of producing the most unexpected events overnight.

This Empire, which had never had a capital, nor any real central force, now began to form new central points in its larger provinces. It was mainly

At Potsdam, near Berlin, the Soldier-King, Frederick-William I, organised an élite army. This illustration shows an officer and a grenadier of the Rothe-Leibbataillon of Potsdam (about 1730).

Brandenburg-Prussia and Austria which attempted to fill the empty place left by the Empire, through a union of their powers. The German dualism between emperor and princes brought about a new form of rivalry between the Habsburg and Hohenzollern houses. This duel determined Germany's internal history and led finally to the liquidation of the First Reich.

After the Thirty Years' War, the leadership of the Brandenburg house was taken over by the twenty-year-old Elector Frederick-William, who later went down into history as the "Great Elector" (1640–1688). He had managed to gain certain lands around the Rhine from the war—Cleves, Mark and Ravensburg. Now he organised an army, because he knew that only brute force was of value. He was strong enough to drive the Swedes out of Germany, and at the Battle of Fehrbellin (1675) he gained part of Pomerania and obtained access to the Baltic. Next he removed the fetters of Polish supremacy from East Prussia and united his Brandenburg territory with this now sovereign land. When he added Emden to his gains, he even founded a Navy, and, with his success on the Gold Coast and in Bengal, began to compete with the major maritime Powers of the day. The Electorate, supported by such expansion of its lands and by an excellent standing army, won great regard in the north and great prestige as a possible ally.

Frederick I's ambition would not be satisfied with the title of Elector. With the agreement of the Emperor, who needed the support of the Brandenburg regiments for the imminent War of the Spanish Succession, Frederick had himself crowned King on his sovereign soil at Königsberg (18 January 1701). Thus the Empire had not only an Emperor in Vienna, but also a King in Prussia. The contrapuntal theme of rivalry and dualism had been introduced.

Frederick William I (1713–1740), the "Soldier King", knew perfectly well that the time would have to come when this rivalry would be asserted with weapons, and he was convinced that on this earth, and especially on the exposed north-German plain, only military strength could decide the lasting existence of a state. Thus he steadily assembled his *"lange Kerls"*, gathered regiment on regiment and had them trained, disciplined and drilled into machines by his old friend Dessauer; he lived a thrifty, Spartan life and poured guilders upon guilders into his future war treasury.

His son, Frederick II (1740–1786), who was later known as Frederick the Great, was to need this war fund, and also the hard upbringing which he endured. For a short time the two courts considered the idea of marrying off the heirs to the two rival houses—that is, Frederick II of Prussia and Maria Theresa, the last of the Habsburgs to stem from Austrian stock. However, this plan dissolved into a thousand in-

The Prussian soldier was subjected to an iron discipline. For the slightest offense he was beaten, broken on the wheel, beheaded or condemned to forced labor. Engravings by Daniel Chodowiecki.

trigues. In 1740, when the succession arose in both lands, war broke out immediately. Those European nations and German princes who had confirmed Maria Theresa's right of succession by supporting the "Pragmatic Sanction", attacked the Austro-Hungarian landmasses in the hope of acquiring parts of these for themselves. Frederick of Prussia was the first to join this free-for-all: he demanded the Silesian dukedoms for himself, on the grounds that his succession allowed for this, and marched his father's highly-drilled army onto the battlefield.

After three terrible, devastating Silesian Wars, the last of which, the Seven Years' War, drove him to the verge of ruin and brought Austria's Russian allies to Berlin, he finally defeated a great coalition of his enemies and acquired Silesia. In this way the Prussians broke the German hold over the Czechs in Bohemia. From then on, Bohemian-Czech nationalism, with support from the north, grew against the Habsburg house. Frederick the Great's Seven Years' War became embroiled in a world war, which England was waging against the French colonial empire. Prussia became England's continental support-force. When Frederick defeated the French at Rossbach on 5th November 1757, he not only helped England to win the war, but also, for the first time since the Thirty Years' War, stirred up Germany's own national feeling. Even Goethe in Frankfurt was at that time pro-Frederick. From the point of view of German politics, any victory against the Emperor and Empire was only an advantage for the spirit of provincialism and for the princes. One must consider that in the Battle of Leuthen alone, the German nation as a whole lost

6000 men on the Prussian side and 25000 on the Austrian side, for the sole purpose of transferring the ownership of one small German province from one princely house to another, whereas on the same day in India, the English gained control of a whole subcontinent, losing only 17 Britons and killing 5000 Indian sepoys.

Once Prussia had successfully asserted itself as a kingdom, Frederick swore not to undertake any more dangerous campaigns. His achievements for Prussia were considerable. As an enlightened, philosophical king, a friend of Voltaire, he was the first of the German princes to introduce an Edict of Tolerance and abolish torture.

When he acquired the totally devastated lands of Western Prussia, and also new areas in the east (after the division of Poland), he turned his energies to draining the swamplands of the Oder and Netze areas, and the development of agriculture. He carried out a policy of potato planting, as a result of which there has never been a hunger problem in Prussia. Following the French mercantile system, he revived the craft industries, developed other industries and trade, organised a finance system, and diligently collected in his taxes to maintain the 200,000-strong standing army.

Intellectual life also found a patron in him. He created his Berlin Academy completely in the popular French image, he also furthered the interests of universities and schools. He was exactly what he claimed to be: "the first servant of the state", an enlightened despot and free-thinker, who, apart from philosophy, believed only in the sword and money.

He was not a great *German*, however. His successful struggle against Austria, and therefore against the im-perial Crown, had served only to increase the disintegration of both Empire and nation, and create the reason for the division of Germany, which was to take place a hundred years later. Frederick II also destroyed the nation's last chance of consolidation and imperial power in 1785, by using military threats and founding a "League of German Princes". He was terested only in the security and growth of Prussia.

At that time plans existed, which, if they had been allowed to be carried out, would probably have renewed the imperial Crown and secured the Empire from the east and west. Bavaria was the third largest province

*Below: Frederick II receiving his brother-in-law in his Masonic lodge.
Opposite page, top: allegorical illustration of the Peace of Hubertsburg
(1763).
Below: "Old Fritz", shortly before his death, on the terrace of the castle
of Sans-Souci.*

after Prussia and Austria, and its elector, Max Emanuel, had tried during the War of Spanish Succession to turn his province into a great independent Power, but had been pitifully crushed by the two great forces. In 1777 the Wittelsbach dynasty died out and Bavaria was united with the Palatinate under Charles Theodor. This fun-loving individual, had been reluctant to leave his residence at Heidelberg–Mannheim for the *"Spiessbürger"* atmosphere of Munich. He was therefore very receptive to the secret plans of his chancellor, Kreitmeyer, and of the imperial court chancellery, who suggested that he should yield Bavaria to Austria, and in return create for himself a great western kingdom from the Palatinate, the Austrian Netherlands and the scat-

tered Austrian possessions along the upper Rhine. The Empire would have been able to present a stronger front against France, Austria would have gained some of the German national strength, and they would have been able finally to fulfil Prince Eugene's plans for resettling the vast expanses of land between the Danube and the Black Sea, areas whose population had been largely wiped out during the Turkish Wars. Frederick II of Prussia could not bring himself to accept these upheavals, which would have left the Emperor in a much stronger position. A stronger Emperor would almost certainly have demanded the return of Silesia, and would have overshadowed Prussia's glory. So, with one foot already in the grave, he once more led his army onto the battlefield,

went as far as Prague, and made sure that the old order of things remained.

Under his successors, his army and administration quickly fell into ruin. Prussia rested on the laurels it had won at the battles of Rossbach and Leuthen, and in 1806 fell a prey to Napoleon. However, the strength and Spartan simplicity which the great king had developed in his people, lived on after their defeat, and provided the impetus for a national revival. This nation of soldiers, peasants and burghers, who had learned once more to be self-aware and German, refused to submit. They became the nucleus of resistance when the French emperor subjected Europe to the supremacy of his army. The impulse for Germany's freedom-fight came from Prussia.

A prince from the Habsburg-Austrian dynasty was still wearing the imperial crown. But Leopold I (1658–1705) had neither the power nor the will to protect this patchwork-quilt of an empire. He had a passive nature, was full of scientific and artistic tendencies, and was more concerned with the fate of his own Austrian dynasty than with the vague concept of Germany. The Empire watched almost helplessly as the French took possession of lands in the west, and made their way towards Caesar's natural frontier, the Rhine. As the French generals rampaged across the Rhineland-Palatinate, the Emperor had other worries. Heidelberg was burned down and its beautiful Renaissance castle was blown up and destroyed; in Mannheim the inhabitants were forced to help destroy their own city; Worms, apart from its cathedral, was reduced to ruins, and in Speier the French chased out the inhabitants, set fire to the city and cathedral, ridiculing the mortal remains of the Salian kings.

While all this was happening, a Turkish army appeared before the walls of Vienna. The Emperor called the princes and the Western world to his aid. A relief army marched in and freed the imperial city in 1683.

In pursuit of the retreating Turks, Austro-imperial politics turned eastwards. The results of the Turkish War began to center on the Balkans. Behind the "Blue Elector" (Max Emmanuel of Bavaria) and "Turkish Louis" (Ludwig of Baden), there now arose the greatest military commander and statesman that the Habsburg dynasty ever produced—Prince Eugene of Savoy.

When the victorious German army forced the Turkish army to retreat far beyond Belgrade, liberated Hungary,

73

between the Leitha Mountains and the Black Sea. That was the time when the German nation should have seized its opportunity to expand.

The Austrian dynasty, just like the Hohenzollern dynasty in Prussia, was striving to increase its own power. When the last of the Habsburgs died on the Spanish throne, fullscale war broke out between all European Powers, over the division of the Spanish inheritance. The battlefields where German armies were involved lay between Turin, Oudenarde, Malplaquet and Höchstädt-Blenheim. The peasants were hit particularly hard when their lands were occupied by Austrian troops, once their own elector, Max Emmanuel, had fled. The peasants of Oberland arose in vain against the Pandurs and Croats. They were de-

Transylvania and later Banat, the nation once more, after a long absence, opened up the way for expansion to the east.

Here in the east lay the new living-space for the overcrowded peasants of Swabia, the Rhineland and Franconia, for the hard-working laborers, who, for various reasons, were refused membership of the city guilds, and for the burghers who had the courage to resettle in foreign lands. Prince Eugene himself drew up the plans for Austria's new turn to the east, and with it, the expansion of Germany.

The emigration of Swabians to Banat, and the settlement of Germans from the Empire in the lower Danube area and Transylvania, began during Maria Theresa's reign. When the Habsburg dynasty, Prussia and Russia divided up the ruined Polish kingdom between them, new, enormous realms came with it.

However, these plans and dreams never became a strong, concrete real-

ity. For decades, the boats from Ulm carried German settlers, with their household belongings and cattle, down the Danube, but money was short, government support was lacking, and there was no real mass emigration of the Germans. Thus, instead of huge settlements, there arose in the east only small German enclaves, national islands, lost outposts of the German nation.

The continuing chain of great wars, with the resulting shortage of money, and the return of political interest to the west, prevented the last possible migration of the German people. Two hundred years later, when Hitler's army marched into Polish territory and as far as the Black Sea, to create living space for the *"Volk ohne Raum"*, it was too late. By this time these areas were occupied by Slavs and Hungarians who had become aware of their national identity. At the end of the Turkish Wars there were only one million people living

feated at the Christmas massacre of Sendling in 1705.

The area had scarcely had time to recover from the horrors of this war, when it became involved in the wars of the Austrian and Bavarian, successions. The Inn area was forfeited, and the people were prevented, by the League of Princes, from joining forces with their native Austria.

The Austrian dynasty was weakened after the wars against Prussia. As the Habsburg dynasty continued to be France's trauma, and the Emperors were resisting the French kings' policies for the Rhine, the policy of this western Power now turned once more against Austria. The unnatural alliance with France against Prussia had been short-lived. It was only pitifully restored later, through the marriage of the Austrian Emperor's daughter, Marie Antoinette, to Louis XVI. Austria remained France's main enemy, and Austria's politics, caught up between France and Prussia, only rarely found the strength to represent the interests of Germany as a whole over the question of the Rhine and Maas areas. In this situation, just as the rival German powers were regarding each other suspiciously, the Empire was divided up into hundreds of small sovereignties, and while the imperial army consisted of nothing more than a rabble of wounded soldiers and ragamuffins, revolution broke out in Paris. New ideas of liberty, human rights, fraternity and equality rose up like flames, and their sparks fell on the tinder-wood of ancient German towns along the Rhine.

After the execution of the royal family in Paris, a coalition of European Powers was formed under the leadership of Emperor Leopold, against revolutionary France. Carried away by their ideas of liberty, the people threw themselves into a wild form of nationalism. The men of Paris announced the *"levée en masse"*—the first-ever general, compulsory military service, a complete mobilization of a whole nation.

At Valmy, where Goethe was an eye-witness, the feudal mercenary armies met for the first time with a national army, and were defeated. Germany retreated from the face of revolution, the French generals moved into the Rhineland.

The seeds of freedom were now sown in this area too, the revolution-

ary *"Carmagnole"* was danced, and liberty was preached. The idea of revolution was discussed in the alehouses of German towns; societies and unions were formed, people's academies thrived. Many people looked expectantly across the Rhine, where a new age seemed to have been born.

A "Robespierre on horseback" emerged from France: Napoleon Bonaparte. He led the banners of the revolutionary armies, along with their ideas of liberty, equality and fraternity, across the French borders. The Austrian armies in Italy, Switzerland and on the Rhine were defeated. In France Napoleon I had himself made Emperor. This was the signal for the end of the German Empire—for the Western World could only tolerate one Caesar. The imperial crown on Napoleon's head indicated a whole program of events: it meant the uniting of Europe under revolutionary ideas and under France's leadership. The ruined German Empire was forced to look on powerless as its fate was decided for it. With the Peace of Luneville (1801), France finally achieved what Caesar had advised for her, and what Louis XIV had sought to obtain for her—that is, her natural frontiers. The valleys of the Rhine and Etsch were from now on to form the frontier with Germany. The German princes who were thereby deprived of their possessions were to be recompensed with secularized Church lands and imperial towns, as well as direct

imperial territories. Thus Napoleon brought to the Germans an end to their multiple small states and the first steps towards national unity.

The Diet of Regensburg approved these arrangements with its Imperial Deputation: *Reichsdeputationshauptausschuss*, and the princes fought like wolves over the free towns, monasteries, ecclesiastical lands, bishoprics and charitable foundations. Only six free towns—Hamburg, Bremen, Lübeck, Frankfurt, Nuremberg and Augsburg—remained provisionally independent. The Church had ceased to possess lands anywhere, ancient cathedrals were destined to be pulled down, their estates were given away, their libraries converted to state libraries, and irreplaceable works of art were sold for ridiculously low prices. "Enlightenment" and profit-seeking won the day.

This aspect of the new times was also revealed in German areas. Freemasons and "enlightened orders" had arisen; suddenly it was considered "intellectual" to be a "free-thinker"; countless school-teachers carried the revolutionary spirit to the people. Emperor Joseph II (1780–1792) had already, as a spiritual son of the Enlightenment, begun this movement in Austria. He had declared general religious tolerance and banned the Jesuit order, dissolving the 700 monasteries and selling the confiscated ecclesiastical estates, or else using them to build schools. He had forbidden the many pilgrimages and processions, and had even converted the cemeteries to lime-pits. He also, of course, abolished serfdom, introduced equal rights for citizens and gave full doctrinal freedom to the universities. These new ideas now began to have effect and caused considerable upheaval in the years of secularization and mediatization.

However, even these rushed reforms were not able to save the decaying system of sovereign-princes. When the war with Napoleon was renewed, and this standard-bearer of revolution marched with enormous armies against Germany, he did not meet with the resistance of an indignant nation. He was greeted rather as a liberator. The princes' enlisted armies could not hold out against these national armies. Thus Austria was in 1805 again defeated, and in 1809 was defeated a third time; the same fate fell to Prussia in 1806 and 1807, and she was humiliated and divided up.

It was not until this time, when the Germans had French troops occupying their towns and villages, when they saw what little use the "Napoleonic Code" was to them, and when they saw the arbitrary behavior of the victors, that a national move to resistance was aroused. This resistance was expressed in the form of individual uprisings, such as Andreas Hofer's Peasant War in the Tirol, or the Hussar officers' uprising, or in protest pamphlets from the printer, Palm.

Meanwhile, Napoleon had bestowed the title of King on the Electors of Baden and Württemberg—and later also on the Elector of Saxony—thereby formally declaring the dissolution of the German Empire. These "kings by France's grace" entered into the Rhenish Confederation as allies on his side. This brought to an end the imperial status of Francis II. On August 6th, 1806, the Holy Roman Empire of German Nations was dissolved, after 944 years of existence. The Habsburg Emperor, as Francis I, took on the title of Emperor of Austria.

Palm, the printer, was shot; his last pamphlet bore the title: "Germany in its greatest humiliation".

77

Napoleon altered the borders of German provinces at his will. Whenever he needed a kingdom for one of his innumerable favorites, he formed one out of German territory. It was in this way that the Kingdom of Westphalia was formed, or the "Free State of Danzig". Prussia lost a half of its territory: it was left with a mere 2877 square miles of the 5570 it had acquired.

However, this great fall brought about in Prussia the measure of insight which normally precedes a revival. The king called upon Baron von Stein, a modern-thinking man, who was anxious for reform, to govern the state. Stein, a patriot, immediately

undertook an inner revival of the Prussian State, bearing in mind the ideals of the French Revolution, and allowing greater freedom for the subjects. He needed citizens who were dedicated to their state and their fatherland. Thus he, and later his successor, Hardenberg (for he himself had to retreat from Napoleon's fury), finally managed, in 1810, to put an end to hereditary subjection, serfdom and the limitation of citizens' personal rights, and arranged for a system of free trade. He introduced self-government for the towns, and reorganized the whole system of state administration. Under generals Scharnhorst, Gneisenau, Boyen and Clausew-

itz, came the beginnings of a reform for the army: the way was prepared for general military service, and a national army was created out of the machine of the mercenary army. Writers such as Heinrich von Kleist and Friedrich Schiller kindled this powerful spirit of awakening nationalism. Ernst Moritz Arndt wrote his "Spirit of the Times", Fichte made his speeches "To the German Nation", and at Berlin University, founded by Wilhelm von Humboldt, men such as Schleiermacher and Wolff were working. The gymnast Jahn was unflinchingly training the students with pre-military drilling and nationalistic addresses.

This feeling of revival and of a new epoch could also be felt in the imperial provinces: Archduke Charles built up a more mobile army and introduced hunting tactics and pursuit instead of the old, rigid battle procedures; the citizens formed national unions, and Haydn, in his old age, composed his hymn, "God save Emperor Francis", which later became the national anthem. When Metternich came to power, a new, extremely cunning and exceptionally active Prime Minister, the future looked brighter, and the balance with France's power seemed to be complete when the Emperor's daughter, Marie-Louise, married the new-comer.

The Continental Blockade, which Napoleon had introduced as a rigid economic boycott of English goods, also had a crippling effect on Germany. Through the increasing exploitation of her coal, her numerous inventions of working machines, and above all through her newly-discovered energy source, the steam engine, along with all the resources of her world-wide colonial empire, England had, in the past two generations,

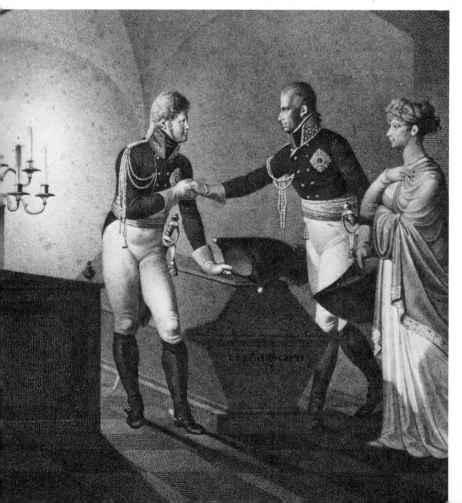

become the chief supplier of the German market. Now all British supplies suddenly dried up. However, the economic crisis and inflation which arose from this also had its positive aspect: in the Ruhr area there developed a whole range of permanent, native industries, in Silesia and the Erzgebirge the weaving industry and cloth mills blossomed forth, and since there was no more cane sugar available, the process of refining sugar from sugar beet was discovered. New branches of industry and trade arose, and the slow change in the German economic structure began.

Defeat, and the occupation of their country, brought about a change in the German national character, which now awoke from its sleepy subjection to a new self-awareness. Thus it was mainly the German provinces which dealt the final blows to Napoleon as he made his way back westwards with his scattered army after the failure of their campaign in the icy Russian winter. The Prussian auxiliary corps, led by York, went over to the Russian side without any direct instructions from the king; Prussia formed a voluntary corps, drafted her men to war service, and stirred up among the population a new storm of enthusiasm for the wars of freedom. Austria entered the fighting with renewed enthusiasm, and even Sweden attacked the French army. After the first battles, it became obvious that Napoleon's glory was on the wane, and even the princes of the Rhenish League forsook him, Bavaria and Württemberg being the first to leave. Only the King of Saxony remained on the side of the French until the final decisive Battle of Leipzig on 16th to 18th October 1813.

The system of a united Europe under French rule was destroyed after Napoleon's military defeat in Russia and Germany. Rebellion had also triumphed in Spain, and the English auxiliary troops began to cross the Pyrenees. In the first night of 1813 the Prussian General Blücher led his

German troops back to the left bank of the Rhine. Prince Schwarzenberg arrived from the south with an Austrian army. The confederates soon reached Paris, Napoleon retreated, and was exiled on the Isle of Elba. In 1814–15 the Czar, Emperor, princes and famous statesmen met in Vienna to try to reorganise the map of Europe which had been so confused and disfigured by revolution and the Napoleonic wars.

All this upheaval and all the catastrophes had taught nobody anything at all. Instead of following the spirit of a new age, establishing a new liberty for the people, and taking advantage of the wave of nationalist feeling aroused by Napoleon, everyone was more concerned with haggling over provinces, cities and peoples, putting the rightful princes back on their lost thrones, and bringing to an abrupt halt any progress which had been achieved by the revolution. The Congress of Vienna danced and celebrated, leaving no doubt at all that the

days of reaction and restoration had arrived. The ordinary people returning from the freedom wars were no longer needed, and had to submit to the rigid discipline of the old systems their hopes for renewal brutally dashed.

Then there was the frightening news of Napoleon's return. The armies had to return to the battlefields. After a hundred days all was decided at the final Battle of Waterloo, south of Brussels. It was Blücher's Prussians who brought victory to the almost-beaten Duke of Wellington, and assured his triumph. Napoleon was banished for ever to the distant Atlantic island of St. Helena. Europe, and with her all the German lands, belonged once more to the re-established dynasties. The hastily-agreed Final Act of the Congress of Vienna established the German Confederation as the replacement for the German Reich. The simplifications which Napoleon had brought to the map of Germany were confirmed in favor of

the larger provinces: Bavaria acquired the Free Cities of Augsburg and Nuremberg, and took on its present-day form; a Kingdom of Hanover emerged, and Prussia, with the help of the Czars, emerged once more as the supreme German power.

In order to protect themselves against any future revolutions, changes, or possible insurrection, the Emperor of Austria, the Czar of Russia and King Frederick William III of Prussia joined together to form the Holy Alliance, whose reactionary spirit was to be the state chancellor, Prince Metternich. A series of subsequent congresses, such as those of Aachen, Troppau, Laibach and Verona, ensured that nothing could change the now solidly-frozen order of Europe. However, in 1815, the number of "sovereign states" had been reduced to 38, as opposed to the 378 which had emerged after the Thirty Years' War; those remaining existed until 1866 as the German Confederation, which loosely bound

Opposite page: the Battle of Leipzig, also known as the Battle of the Nations (October 16–19 1813).
Below: two caricatures of the Congress of Vienna. Talleyrand notices the direction in which the wind is blowing; England is tossed about; the allies waver, the king of Saxony fears for his crown and Genoa jumps for the king of Sardinia. While the Tsar, the Emperor of Austria and the king of Prussia divide Europe, Napoleon looks on from Elba.

them together. Only part of the lands of Prussia and Austria, however, belonged to this confederation.

In place of the old Diet, a *"Bundestag"* (Federal Assembly) now met in Frankfurt; the provincial rulers all sent their representatives, but the voice of the people was not to be heard. Austria presided over the assembly. The constitution now demanded that any decisions taken must be unanimous, so in fact hardly any were taken. There was to be a federal army, federal fortifications, even a German navy, but, here too, no decisive action was taken. Prussia looked on rather sceptically, as she was playing a secondary role, and was convinced, in spite of her achievements at Napoleon's defeat, that she was not adequately rewarded. Even the promise that the individual provinces were to have their own constitutions, and that civil rights were to be decreed, was fulfilled only in some places. The province of Weimar-Saxony, at Goethe's instigation, was the first to receive its own constitution in 1816; then followed Bavaria and Baden in 1818, Württemberg in 1819, and a few smaller provinces.

However, the two great German powers, Prussia and Austria, seemed to be reluctant to take part in the question of constitutions. Above all, Prince Metternich had no intention of yielding the slightest atom of imperial power, but merely permitted the harmless activity of a few provincial assemblies. The obstinate Prussian king took the same attitude. He went against the promise that he had made in his hour of need in 1810, and which he had renewed as long as he needed his subject's support and war service; now, after victory, he allowed the reactionaries around him to triumph, and in 1823, under pressure, he

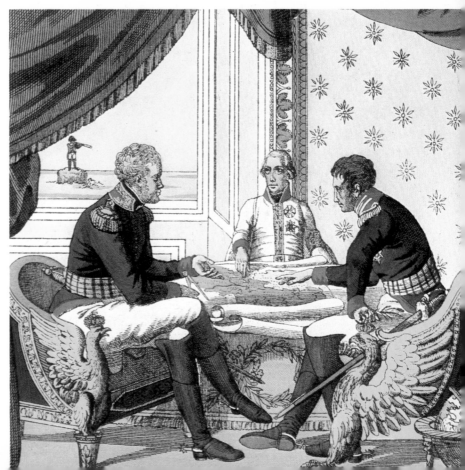

In 1819 the student Karl Ludwig Sand stabbed to death the absolutist writer Kotzebue, who was suspected of being a spy in the pay of the Tsar. Below: rioting in Frankfurt-am-Main, on April 3 1833 (picture by Epinal).

allowed only the most insignificant provincial assemblies to be established. There was to be no parliament, no free elections, no democracy; the population was to remain as it was—totally subjected! The awakened national spirit, the flame of nationalism, which had been kindled against Napoleon, the feeling of patriotism and the desire for liberty, could not be suppressed now that Germany's people were returning home as victors. It had been mainly

the students who had rushed out under the banners of the freedom corps, and now they came back again: they were long-haired, bearded, and dressed in the fanciful Litewka and Dolman outfits, with battle jackets, cockades and daggers, top-boots and spurs. They were the ones who now protested and demonstrated, talking of radical change for the system. Goethe, in the wisdom of his old age, hated as he was for his moderate, emotionless standpoint, scorned these

young world-changers. He wrote in one of his plays the following stage direction: "turning to the audience, where the students are protesting at the tops of their voices:

'Die Welt, sie war nicht, ehe ich sie schuf!
Die Welt zu ändern, das ist mein Beruf!'"
(The world did not exist before I created it!
I am the one to change it!)

And he made fun of a generation which respected neither experience nor old age, and insisting that it knew better:

"Das Alter ist ein kaltes Fieber
ein Frost von greisenhafter Not!
Hat einer erst mal dreissig Jahr vorüber –
es wär am besten – man schlüg' ihn tot!"
(Old age is a cold fever,
the frost of an old man's need!
Once a man has passed the age of thirty,
the best thing is to have him killed!)

The wave of troublesome and rebellious youth strove forcefully for a new liberty and nation.

The Romantic poets dreamed of the times of the emperors and the Reich, newly-founded fraternities and corps trained in the use of weapons; the spirit of the freedom wars was simmering. Associations such as the *"Unbedingten"* (the absolutists) even planned to establish their republic by means of assassination of the tyrants. Great demonstrations took place, such as the one at the Wartburg Castle in 1817, and later the one at Hambach in 1832. A young fanatic murdered the arch-reactionary Kotzebue. Jahn's

On 18 October 1817 the students' societies met in the Wartburg on the occasion of the three-hundredth anniversary of the Protestant Reformation and the fourth anniversary of the Battle of the Nations; this was a great demonstration against the policy of restoration pursued by the Germanic Confederation.

athletes were also in support of the students.

All these events gave Metternich and the Holy Alliance the excuse for passing the Karlsbad Resolutions of 1819. Journals and pamphlets were subjected to strict censorship, the universities were placed under strict surveillance, fraternities and athletic clubs were banned, and a central commission was set up to combat "demagogic machinations". The local rulers began to take a harder line. Students, professors, publishers, poets and philosophers were thrown into prison; Görres could only save himself by fleeing; Schleiermacher, Fichte, even Gneisenau were suspected. Reprinting of Fichte's writings was prohibited. Fritz Reuter was thrown into jail, and the writings of the "Young Germany" movement were seized by the police. When seven professors from Göttingen—among them the Brothers Grimm—refused to take the Oath of Allegiance, they were dismissed and all of Germany's progressive thinkers reached boiling-point. In spite of the Biedermeier period, post carriages, small-town idylls and the ale-house spirit of the German *Spiessbürger*, the times were full of intellectual, political and rebellious unrest.

The effects were being felt of a sharp increase in population, which was affecting the whole of Europe, but which reached special peaks in Germany. In spite of the wars which had

gone before and the cholera which had been carried in by the Cossacks during the Polish Rebellion of 1830–31, the cities were expanding towards their future mass populations. Berlin, which in 1775 had had 135,000 inhabitants, reached 250,000 by 1831. Vienna at that time already had 210 000 people. At first it had been Napoleon's continental embargo which had forced Germany to begin her own industries, but once trade with England had been re-established, the influence of English industry was felt, and factories, mechanical workshops, mines and mass-production lines sprang up in the German provinces. England had developed the steam engine around 1764. The revolutionary inventions of the Spinning Jenny, the mechanical loom, the puddling furnace, turning lathe, gas lighting, steam ship and railways, cast steel and blast furnace revolutionized production methods and conditions and were now used in Germany also. In 1777 Berlin had had just 457 "factories". By 1830 the number had grown to 1653; these were enterprises of the most varied kind, employing some 20,000 workers.

There was already a breed of sweated laborers on the country estates, who were practically without rights or possessions; to these were now added a rapidly-multiplying urban proletariat. The introduction of the railways—Germany's first one linking Nuremberg to Fürth in 1835, then in 1837 Leipzig to Dresden—created new transport routes which brought the various provinces closer together, and which were soon able to provide fast links between industrial areas and their markets.

Goethe once remarked to his secretary, Eckermann, who was con-

cerned about Germany's political fate and her disunity: "Oh! Don't worry; whatever the politicians fail to do will be achieved by our good old railways." This nation once again experienced the most luxuriant growth and fruition of its intellectual and cultural life in these times of rigid reaction and the persistent lack of liberty. It is as if the German spirit, when it failed to overcome political and social realities which it abhorred, took refuge in the realm of poetry, the arts, science and invention.

At this time both Schlegels were at work, and also Ludwig Tieck, the philosopher Hegel and his numerous followers. The most significant, of course, and the most productive, was Karl Marx from Trier. Arnim and Brentano were working on their collections of folk-songs, the Grimm brothers on their fairy-tale collection. The Romantic poetry of Eichendorff, Schenkendorff, E. T. A. Hoffmann and Chamisso emerged. Grillparzer

was writing his dramatic works, and Uhland, Platen, Rückert and Immermann were writing. Heinrich Heine, critical of his times, lyrical, yet writing with a rebellious and political tendency, was pouring forth his songs, epic poems and defamatory attacks on German petty-bourgeois society. Hoffmann von Fallersleben renewed interest in the folk-song form, and gave the nation the song which was later to become the national anthem.

The Romantic period found its strongest expression in painting. Overbeck, Caspar David Friedrich, Schwind and the Nazarenes were alive. The cool Classical works of Cornelius, Schadow, Gärtner, Klenze, Rauch, Schinkel and Rietschel competed with the Romantics. In the sphere of music, Germany also asserted its lead. The songs of Franz Schubert or Robert Schumann could be heard during these decades, and the operas of Carl Maria von Weber and Heinrich Marsch were popular.

85

Meyerbeer, Mendelssohn and other great musicians appeared. In the sciences people were discussing the achievements of the Germanists and the prolific talents of the Humboldt brothers. Among historians the names of Niebuhr, Ranke and Dahlmann were establishing themselves, and in the realm of jurisprudence, Savigny, Haller and Rotteck were the famous names; the national economy boomed through the genius of Frederick List. It was at this time that Kirchhoff discovered spectral analysis, and Bunsen developed this new field of science; the German astronomer Herschel, working from English observatories, opened up new realms of the heavens, and Justus von Liebig discovered the bases of plant nutrition, thus opening up the way to modern agriculture. Gauss gave us the

telegraph, and König and Bauer invented the high-speed printing-machine; even the sewing machine, four-color printing, the typewriter and hundreds of other new mechanical aids were born in those small German towns which were caught up in the net of reactionary restoration and dreaming their way towards freedom.

Censorship, police rule and harsh legal sentences had served only to dampen the students' movement, the intellectuals and the journalists, but had not been able to silence them. It is evident particularly in the example of Heinrich Heine that literature had undergone a radical change: there had been progress from Romanticism, art and fanaticism to criticism, dissociation and political thinking. The representatives of this "Young Germany" movement now took on a

radical tone, and the reactionary groups gave them more and more cause. The struggle to obtain better conditions of civil liberty in the individual states became more and more earnest, and beside this there emerged the demand for a new reorganization of Germany as a *whole*. Everyone realized the attitude of the Church to this struggle, and was aware of the well-known link between Church and throne; the new movement turned against the Church and its hierarchy, as was shown in the tumult at Trier in 1844. Added to all this was the desperate position of the working proletariat, particularly in the Hunger Year, 1847. The pamphlets of Marx and Engels were coming across from Paris, Brussels and London. The troubles took on socialist and communist tendencies in some proletarian circles. The bourgeoisie, growing more aware of its own position, was demanding greater democracy.

Thus the time was ripe for a radical change to upset the old order of things.

In the meantime, the power-sharing in German lands had taken a turn in Prussia's favor. The north-German trade association, founded in 1818, had developed into the German Customs Union *(Zollverein)*, and in 1834 Bavaria and Württemberg joined it. This formed a strong economic bond which linked the German provinces, and produced a model for a viable political unity.

The old imperial power of Austria was excluded, and watched as German dualism deposed Vienna from its historic role of leadership, and replaced it with Berlin.

When, in 1848, the news of the February Revolution in Paris reached Germany, this movement, which was primarily a democratic movement led by the bourgeoisie, met with great sympathy. Immediately, on the day after the Paris uprising, there were public meetings and demonstrations in the town of Offenburg. The people were demanding freedom for the press, assize courts, civil defence and a German parliament. The old freedom flag of the Peasant Wars was hoisted—the black, red and gold. When the government of Baden gave in to the demands of the Offenburg mobs, similar things happened in other provinces such as Württemberg, Hesse-Darmstadt, Kurhesse, Hanover and Saxony—the leaders of the liberal opposition were called to the government buildings. In Munich there was student and burgher unrest. King Ludwig I—the artistic founder of the new Munich, abdicated and transferred the reins of government into the hands of Crown-Prince Maximilian. In Vienna the revolt of the masses swept away the reactionary chancellor, Prince Metternich. The old order was breaking up. The numerous unemployed members of the proletariat streamed into Vienna to give the revolution a socialist aspect, and chased the Emperor into exile at Innsbruck.

Just as turbulent were the March days in Berlin, where there were 14-hour street battles and barricades. In this hour of chaos the Prussian king declared that he would rule as a constitutional monarch and lead Germany as a free, united nation. A Prussian National Assembly met to draw up a constitution.

However, by this time there were certain radical movements, especially in Baden, Rhineland-Palatinate and southern Swabia, whose leaders, such as Hecker and Struve, were demanding a German *republic*.

On 5th March, south-German

delegates of the Federal Assembly met in Heidelberg to form a pre-parliament, which was to meet in Frankfurt on 31st March and demand free, general elections for the formation of a National Assembly. The ever-popular Archduke John of Austria presided over the conference in Frankfurt, where a new constitution was called for, to be preceded by a statement of basic rights.

The Frankfurt Parliament, whose members included many writers, professors and liberals, debated endlessly the subject of "Greater or Lesser Germany", in other words a Germany with or without Austria. Those in favor of a "Lesser Germany", who wanted to bestow upon the King of Prussia the hereditary title of Emperor, were especially successful after the October Events in Vienna. Meanwhile the Austrian Emperor's lands and provinces had sunk into the turmoil of revolution: Hungary, Italy, the Slavonic areas were all combining their freedom fight with a feeling of national concern. The Austrian officials and military men had to quit almost all of their positions. In Vienna itself, a wild mob forced its way into the War Ministry and murdered Minister Latour. The Emperor was horrified and left the capital. He let his generals loose on the people; these generals were led by the harsh extremist, Radetzky. This led to harsh repression in Italy. Hungary defended herself under the leadership of Kossuth, but the czar joined forces with Radetzky and sent in his Cossacks, who cruelly suppressed all revolution and liberty. In Prague, Prince Windischgrätz created order, General Jellachich and Windischgrätz marched towards Vienna, took the city, and carried out severe reprisals. The Emperor resigned and gave over the government to his nephew, Francis Joseph (1848–1916). This new monarch "granted" the country a constitution.

The Frankfurt Parliament elected, by 267 votes to 263, to offer the imperial dignity to King Frederick William IV of Prussia. The Prussian, however, refused to accept a crown from a people's "revolutionary" parliament—he wanted to hold the crown by divine right.

The forces of reaction and aristocracy had by this time recovered from the shock, and were uniting once more. The larger federal provinces recalled their representatives from Frankfurt. The parliament had to flee to Stuttgart, where it was dissolved by the Württemberg minister, Römer on 18th June 1849.

Prussian regiments now entered Baden and the Rhineland Palatinate to complete the operation; Austria established order on her own soil. The revolution was over, many freedom-fighters were shot, others were imprisoned, and others fled to America in search of freedom and democracy. The subsequent negociations between the states only served to re-establish the Confederacy in its earlier form. The year 1848 had also witnessed the birth of Karl Marx' and Engels' Communist Manifesto. It became evident that there was a proletarian movement which longed for a socialistic republic and a total upheaval of the existing society. The cells of a workers' movement were forming in Germany.

The hopes of the German people had yet again come to nothing. The revolutionary fire was still smoldering in the hearts of the bourgeoisie, the intellectuals and the workers, but the nation's condition was just as lamentable as before. In the larger provinces, such as Prussia, Bavaria and Austria, the reactionary factions sought to win back their lost positions. The Church strengthened her alliance with the thrones and secured her powerful position by means of concordats. The more liberal ministers had to give way to the more reactionary ones, new restrictions were imposed on the press, political associations were placed under strict surveillance, and the constitutions were pruned of all their libertarian clauses. The fate of Germany returned to the hands of the two rival states: Prussia and Austria.

The King of Prussia, in his hour of danger, had called upon a reactionary landed proprietor to be his minister; his name was Otto von Bismarck. This man cast aside and dissolved the Diet (Landtag), used his great diplomatic skill to create for himself a prominent position in the parliament (Bundestag), to which he was sent as Prussian envoy, and soon became the key political figure of the times. He stood beside William, who, until 1861 reigned under the title of Prince Regent, and furthered very consciously Prussian aims and interests: he considered Germany to be nothing more than a potential area for the extension and expansion of Prussian-Hohenzollern power.

Austria emerged from these years of revolution both inwardly and outwardly weakened, so it was not surprising that she now soon lost the battle in the final stages of this dualism. In 1859 she had to grant Italy her "freedom as far as the Adriatic", after which, in 1861, Italy declared herself a kingdom under Victor Emmanuel of Savoy. In Prussia, Bismarck had been sent as envoy to St. Petersburg to negotiate Prussia's future rear cover in the east, and had also taken part in the suppression of a Polish rebellion; strengthened by these achievements, he was now called upon by King Wil-

liam to be his minister. In 1863, at the Congress of Princes in Frankfurt, he assumed the decisive role against Austria. In 1864 there was war with Denmark over the German princedoms of Schleswig-Holstein, and Prussia entered the fighting with the assistance of the imperial house, since it was a federal or imperial matter. It was, however, the Prussian troops who won the victories. At first, Prussia and Austria administered the conquered princedoms jointly, but this arrangement soon brought conflict. Bismarck was waiting for the right moment, and when Austria was weak and involved in differences with Hungary and Italy, he declared war. At the same time he formed a secret alliance with Italy, and applied to the *Bun-*

destag for the formation of a directly and generally-elected parliament, for the purpose of bringing about a federal reform. In spite of this, most of the south-German federal states still held to the old imperial house of Austria. The weak federal troops were defeated; General Helmut von Moltke won the decisive Battle of Königsgrätz (3rd June 1866) against Austria. The imperial troops' victory over the Italians at Custozza was to no avail. Only a few weeks later, Vienna had to sign the Peace of Prague.

Only the south-German provinces retained their independence, and had to form a "defensive and offensive alliance" with Prussia. In north Germany Prussia rounded off her territories by incorporating Reuss, Han-

over, Hesse-Kassel, Nassau and the free city of Frankfurt. All states north of the river Main entered the North German Confederation. On 24th February 1867 a constitutional *Reichstag* met, and immediately decided that all lands to the north of the Main would represent one federal territory with joint political and economic institutions. The King of Prussia was to have the federal presidency and full executive powers.

The traditional imperial power of Austria was thereby excluded from the German *Reich*, and those in favor of the "Lesser Germany" solution to the problem had won. Bismarck was made a count and became the first chancellor of the Confederation (*Bundeskanzler*).

90

"Force rules over law", a French caricature denouncing Krupp and his empire after the end of the 1870–71 Franco-German War.

For a long time France had been a leading opponent of the empire and of Austria; Napoleon III, the Bonapartist who had risen to the status of dictator in the new empire, had done all he could to weaken the Habsburg empire. Now he realized that in doing so, he had helped a new, much more vigorous opponent into the seat of power. The Rhineland which he longed to recapture was forbidden to him, since the great Prussian power was waiting beyond it.

Bismarck knew that France must be his next enemy in war. He could not afford to wait until the French and Austrian armies had had time to rearm with the new needle-guns, cannons and "mitrailleuses", and reorganize their armies better. The conflict came to a head over the question of a Prussian prince as heir to the Spanish throne. The emperor of France spoke out in arrogant words against the candidature of the Prussian, and Prussia withdrew. Bismarck, however, knew how to take advantage of the right moment. He "skilfully mutilated" the Ems dispatch, showing the meeting between the old King William and the French ambassador, Benedetti, in such a provocative light, that a wave of anger swept through the German nation. The French nationalists also began to shout for war. To Bismarck's relief, the French declaration of war was handed over on 19th June 1870, just as the *Reichstag* was meeting in Berlin. France had hoped for support from the South Germans, but was disappointed. There were no cries of revenge after the defeat of 1866; on the contrary, the zeal of all Germans over the Rhine issue, and for the unity of the nation, swept aside all political good sense. They started to sing the *"Wacht am Rhein"* (Rhine guard), dressed up in oak leaves, and de-

manded from their government that they fulfil the offensive and defensive alliance with Prussia. Austria, however, was weakened, threatened by Hungary and Italy, and was not ready with her armaments.

Thus the troops of all branches of the German people, except the Austrians, marched onto the battlefield. The new alliance was sealed with blood on the battlefield. Prussian strategy surrounded Napoleon III with his main army at Sedan, whilst a steady stream of Bavarian and other south-German columns penetrated the southern part of France.

Even the desperate national war which France, now a republic, waged against the superior German force, could change nothing in the outcome of the struggle. By the end of 1870 Paris was besieged by German armies.

The *casus belli* had proved conspicuously what German unity was capable of. The work now had to be completed: Germany was not to be bound together by the loose ties of a Confederation—what was required once more was a united empire under a Kaiser. Bismarck's diplomatic skill and the victories in France created this new empire. For months on end there were letters, conferences and secret reports. Bavaria sought for a long time to retain her independent status, and this southern state only came to agreement when Bismarck allowed the Bavarian king, Ludwig II to retain rights over the army, postal services, telegraphs and railways, rights which

Bismarck then had to grant also to the state of Württemberg; Bismarck also paid out a few millions to Ludwig, who used the money to pay off the debts he had incurred through his adventures with Richard Wagner and through the building of his fantastic castles. Bismarck had to struggle for a long time with his friend and battle-companion, King William of Prussia, for the proud king as might have been expected did not wish to accept office from the hands of the people; he wished to be Emperor of Germany rather than German Emperor.

Thus it was that Otto von Bismarck, who had been made a prince and designated Chancellor, stood in the background when William was proclaimed German Emperor at the famous ceremony in the Palace of Versailles. The Emperor was sulking, for Bismarck had not achieved all that he wanted.

The people had no idea of the tensions and compromises involved in the establishing of the new Reich; it was sufficient for them that it had finally been achieved. They were to have a freely-elected *Reichstag*, a Germany which could once more play its part in the European power-game, and a free, flourishing state. Even the provinces of Alsace and Lorraine, annexed by Louis XIV, returned now to the German Empire; the millions of francs demanded as war-indemnity, which represented an enormous sum in gold, were to invigorate Germany's industry and economy. The foundations of Germany's future power and glory were now being laid.

The Second Reich had been born, and everyone hoped that it would last for ever. In fact its life-span was limited to 47 years.

8 Splendor and Misery of the Second Reich

The newly-founded federal state had reduced the number of its individual states to 25, which were now joined by the province of Alsace-Lorraine. In addition, two states—Bavaria and Württemberg—claimed special rights for themselves. Each state was represented in the federal council in proportion to its significance and strength, whilst 382 members of the *Reichstag* were elected by the people as a whole in direct, secret, general elections. Parties were now formed for the first time, the new National-Liberal party proving to be the strongest. The newly-acquired state of Alsace-Lorraine was ruled over in dictatorial fashion by the Emperor's viceroy. The presence of Prussian officials and soldiers had the effect of

ensuring that the peoples of these oft-disputed regions never really belonged wholeheartedly or by choice to this young German Empire.

In parliament too, things did not always go as smoothly as Bismarck and Kaiser William I had imagined they would. The young Empire believed that its existence and future depended mainly on its military strength. Bitter experiences had taught Prussia that weakness was a political crime, and that one could not rely upon the loyalty of neighboring states. The memory of the Napoleonic wars and of Louis XIV's predatory wars still lingered in German minds. For this reason Germany maintained, right from the outset, a standing army of 402,000, and also began to build up

an efficient navy. But as time went on the parties became more and more reluctant to grant the taxes which were necessary for these projects.

France had never fully accepted her defeat, and thoughts of revenge were nurtured in schools, newspapers and parliamentary speeches; the French cultivated their hatred of "Prussian militarism" and armed themselves with great zeal. In this way the German Empire developed into a military power, armed to the teeth. This was happening while the Empire was still developing within itself, and was still forming itself into a state. A uniform book of trade and penal laws was issued, and in 1873 a "People's Law Book" *(Bürgerliches Gesetzbuch)* was begun, based on the model of the

"Code Napoleon". For this purpose the Empire created for itself at the Supreme Court of Justice in Leipzig, a higher law-court (1879). The postal service and railways were united and made into national institutions—still, however, respecting the special rights of the states of Bavaria and Württemberg. In 1878 the German post-master-general even brought into being the World Postal Association. Added to all these organizations, which served to make Germany appear to be a political unit in the eyes of the world outside, was the uniform weights and measures system, and then the monetary unit, the *Reichsmark* brought uniformity to her gold currency.

The Second Reich was a state governed by the nobility, officers, land-owners and proprietors. The greatly-expanded proletarian class, the laborers and farm workers regarded the social structure at first with distrust, later with aversion. After an initial ban on all workers' associations, during the sixties the printers and metal-workers of Prussia had formed trade unions, and by 1880 these had an enormous, and ever-increasing following. By 1863 Ferdinand Lassalle had already given a political form to the scientifically-based social theses of Marx and Engels. Lassalle died in a duel in 1864, and in 1866 Karl Marx published his main work, "Das Kapital"; in 1869 Bebel and Liebknecht constituted at Eisenach the German Social Democrat Party, which was formed out of the General German Workers' Union.

The new party demanded that a free people's state be established, with equal voting rights for all, including women, from the age of twenty. They wanted the people to have the right to make laws, administer justice and decide the issues of war and peace; they wanted freedom of the press and religion, freedom to belong to associations of their choosing, and establish legal control over working hours.

Bismarck's future opposition grew out of this working class which the Empire scarcely acknowledged as its own. First of all, however, Bismarck became involved in a conflict with the Catholic Church.

In Rome it had not been forgotten that it was Bismarck who had given the green light to the Italian Confederation which had taken control of the Church State in 1870. In "Ultramontanist" circles it was estimated that, within the Empire, the leading power was not a Protestant one. Thus, under the leadership of Bishops Ketteler, Windhorst and others, the Catholic Centre Party was formed. This party demanded the total independence of the Church from the State. Bismarck, however, had taken into his protection certain teachers, professors and clerics who had refused to recognize the "Infallibility of the Pope", which had been proclaimed in 1870; this

group of people had been disciplined by the Bishops, and partly on their account, Bismarck became involved in a harsh campaign against the Catholic Center and Church, the *Kulturkampf*, which lasted for almost eight years. The Center and the Ultramontanists in Bavaria were given solid support by other dissatisfied elements, such as the Welfs and the Danish and Polish minorities. The *Reichstag* voted a *Kanzelparagraph*, a law governing the inspection of schools, and a ban on the Jesuit Order. In 1874 civil marriage was made obligatory, and in the following year a law was published which prevented disobedient priests from receiving their fees. In spite of all these measures, by 1874 the Center had increased its number of deputies from 58 to 92, and in the next elections their numbers rose to 106.

It was only after the death of the obstinate Pope Pius IX that any form of settlement could be envisaged. Meanwhile the Social Democrats had gained in strength. In the first *Reichstag* there had only been two socialist deputies, but the third one voted 12 of them in. In 1873 the economic explosion which had been brought about by the millions of francs gained from the French in war reparation, fizzled out, and a crisis set in, which caused many firms to close down. Workers, and especially now the unemployed, were extremely hard hit. The legislative anarchy which always worked in favor of the rich factory-owners and employers, and permitted all forms of exploitation and abuse of men by men, had created a social vacuum, and brought more and more people flocking to join the workers' party. The ruling classes looked upon this process with apprehension and were grateful when they were given the occasion to intervene with harsh action. On 11th May 1878 a young fanatic, a degenerate pedlar of Social Democrat newspapers, called Hödel, fired some shots at the ageing Kaiser. He failed to hit the emperor, but had struck a fatal blow at his own party. A few days later a certain Dr. Nobiling aimed with greater accuracy at the Kaiser; this time, it was apparently the work of a madman, but the government was indifferent to the culprit.

The government took the opportunity of rushing through very strict anti-socialist laws. These events all served to focus attention on the economic condition of the Empire.

A great change had taken place in the Empire. This nation, which had once lived from agriculture, craftsmanship and trade, had become truly industrial. The huge market created now by the unity of the Empire and by her free-trade policy, modelled on English methods, brought about the building of more and more factories. However—as the German Commissioner at the World Exhibition at Melbourne so rightly pointed out—German products were cheap and poor.

The crisis of 1873 brought manufacturers to the decision that only quality articles could survive on the world market. From then on, German firms struggled to produce only the best, so that the trademark "Made in Germany", introduced as an answer to England's furious, jealous competition, became a much sought-after symbol in the world markets.

Supported by this flourishing industry, Bismarck introduced indirect taxes, the tobacco and brandy monopoly, thus acquiring the money to arm an army of 500,000 men and to built up a naval fleet. He was shrewd enough to give in to the social demands of the working classes, and embarked upon a scheme of social legislation, thereby silencing the masses for a while. Laws which had been passed in 1871 were no longer sufficient to ensure the living rights of the lower classes, and in view of the rapidly-developing industry and the obvious exploitation of the work-force by its employers, society, state and Church began to take their responsibilities more seriously. The outlines of a social policy were presented to the *Reichstag* in 1881 by an imperial representative. Sickness and accident insurance were introduced for workers, and later came the old-age and invalid pensions. In this way Germany became the first of the industrial states to have laws governing a social security system.

All this, of course, did not stop the socialists' efforts; in 1891, at their party conference in Erfurt, they outlined an improved program. By 1912 the SPD had gathered $4^1/2$ million voters. The Anarchists were not silenced by Bismarck's social reforms either: in 1883 there was an attempt to blow up the Kaiser and a gathering of princes. Soon after this, the police chief in charge of the inquiry into this crime was shot. In spite of this, the anti-socialist laws, which expired in 1890, were not renewed. The Empire learned to live with the Socialists.

The growing German economy began to look more and more towards the outside world. Germany had been very late to join the ranks of the great world Powers, and had slept through the age of colonial empires. She only laid her claim at the last minute, when there only remained barren deserts, jungles and remote islands. In 1882 the German Colonial League was founded, and in 1884 the empire took over protectorates in south-west Africa. In 1883 Luderitz, a trader from Bremen, had bought territories in this part of the world. Then, in 1884, the explorer, Gustav Nachtigal negotiated sovereign power over Togoland and the Cameroons for the Empire.

The settlement of the German South-Seas Colonial League on various groups of islands in the north-east of New Guinea was carried out under imperial protection. Finally, in 1885, the German East-African Company was formed, and negotiated for large areas of territory from the Sultan of Zanzibar.

A German Colonial Empire came into being. Her colonies were widely scattered and could only be brought to any semblance of civilization by an enormous amount of hard work, but they were large enough to anger the old-established colonial powers. By 1914 England owned about one quarter of the world's surface, France held about one-eighth, Russia one-sixth: Germany entered the race with only one-twentieth. The competition was for raw materials, markets and strategic military bases. In 1886 Germany called for a Congo Conference, which met in Berlin to establish definite territorial limits in Africa, and to lay down conditions of ownership; it was decreed that in the event of a war in Europe, the colonies should not be mobilized to fight for any European country, and should not take part in any way. Twenty-eight years later, when the First World War broke out, it emerged that Germany was the only country to have held to this agreement: apart from defence troops she had no armies, no military bases and no naval bases in her colonies.

Gradually, signs of tension were once more building up between the Great Powers. Germany's rapid rise to industrial, economic and military power had not gone unnoticed, and was viewed with apprehension in Europe. France clung to her vindictive chauvinism and dreamed of revenge; England realised with distrust and

anger that a new competitor was threatening her markets, that German colonies were getting in the way of some of her colonial designs (German East Africa, for example, broke England's line from the Cape to Cairo), and Germany's growing naval and merchant fleets were threatening England's supremacy on the seas. The Russian Empire of the Czars, on whose reserve Bismarck had once based his policies, had, ever since the Berlin Congress in 1872, been growing away from Germany. A second Berlin Congress, in 1878, at which Bismarck's machinations had tried to establish a European balance of power in the Balkans and the East, had not satisfied the Russians. In spite of this he managed to negotiate a secret Reinsurance Treaty with Russia—a treaty which William I then irresponsibly neglected to renew.

In addition, Germany had formed

an alliance with Italy in 1883, and thus believed that she had nothing to fear from France's dreams of revenge and England's mounting jealousy.

Then came the year 1888, when the old Emperor William I died, followed 99 days later by the death of his son and heir. A whole generation was thus missed out, and the title of Kaiser passed to the very young grandson, William II (1888–1918). He was to be a well-intentioned, idealistic and romantic Kaiser, a Wagnerian hero-type, a hotshot full of emotion, fine phrases, heroic deeds and over-compensatory fears. All too often he hid his personal and political fears behind wild speeches, foolish threats and much waving of his saber. William II soon came into conflict with Bismarck, since his youthful sense of insecurity led him to insist on his undisputed role of ruler, and led him to fear the presence of any great political figure near

to him. On 20th March 1890 he dismissed the ageing chancellor. England's "Punch" magazine showed a cartoon with the caption: "The old pilot goes overboard". William II insisted that, from then on, HE was going to govern Germany.

Although the young ruler strove earnestly to imitate the devotion to duty and the resolute determination of his paragon, Frederick the Great, he succeeded in alienating all his political partners because of his inertia, his theatrical behavior, his blustering battle-cries and his weakness.

He treated the working classes with complete lack of understanding, and answered their demands with massive threats, so that in 1912 the SPD became the strongest party with 110 deputies. He upset the middle classes, especially in the southern regions of the Empire, with his ostentatious love of pomp, show, nobility, the officer-classes and all things military.

At the same time the Empire was thriving and her success became more and more obvious. By 1891 the population had exceeded 41 million, which increased to 68 million by 1914. The annual national income reached 40 billion gold marks, and the total national assets were estimated at over 300 billion. With such power behind him, the Kaiser continued to build up and equip his army. Magnificent parades and effective maneuvers were worrying the rest of Europe, who

were gradually learning to fear German militarism. The Kaiser's special protégé was his navy. His Chief Admiral, Tirpitz, had discovered the Risk Theory, that the German navy had to be strong enough to represent a risk for the two combined next-strongest navies. At Kiel battleships were built, which were even superior to the famous English Dreadnought.

With this race to equip his army, and especially his navy, the Kaiser brought upon himself the deadly enmity of all those countries who believed that his activity was directed against them.

The Kaiser made dangerous speeches which incited the foreign press, such as his "we are the salt of the earth". In the Boer War of 1899–1902 he sent a telegram to the Boer President expressing his sympathy for their cause and promising support. This, of course, brought England's enmity upon himself and the Reich. A short time after, however, he volunteered to work out England's plan of campaign against the Boers for

his cousin, Edward VII; he put on the uniform of a British admiral, and behaved more English than the English at the British naval maneuvers.

In the numerous crises which developed between 1900 and 1914 over French interests in Morocco and the Balkan question, he made frequent threats, but failed to act. He looked on powerless as the countries around him began to join forces against him and his empire. In 1904 France and Britain signed the "Entente Cordiale". France also formed an alliance with Russia, and England carried on secret negotiations with possible allies in case of war.

It is clear that England, under Edward VII, was preparing for a showdown with Germany; in 1912, for example, Lord Kitchener and Hussein of Mecca had already held discussions concerning a secret treaty. The terms of the treaty were that if war broke out, the Arabs would march against their caliphs and their Padshah in Istanbul. In return they were promised their own caliphate and the recon-

struction of the Arabian Empire. The Sultan, however, was the ally of the Central Powers, and it was across his flanks that the fatal blow against Germany was finally struck.

The Russians, after their defeat by the Japanese, had turned their attention from the Far East to the West once more, and served to protect the Slavs, especially the Serbians, whose great enemy, Austria, was engaged in the Balkan crisis. Anyone who wanted to destroy Austria could not avoid Germany. Russia wanted to create for herself a passage through to the sea, and to this end needed to capture Königsberg and Danzig. Russia therefore used up all her credit with France in equipping herself with modern military aids.

The whole world was poised on the brink of a highly explosive situation. There was the German Empire with its rather dubious allies, who consisted of Italy (militarily weak and vulnerable to attack from the sea), Austria (a multi-national state which was creaking at the joints), and the decaying

Sultanate on the Bosphorus; on the other side stood a world-wide coalition which was determined to put an end to the saber-rattling and inflammatory speeches of the Kaiser, to the parades and maneuvers of this ostentatious military state, and to the dreams and trade of this powerful new business competitor. In the middle of this complexity of automatic alliances, this mutual fear of the first step, this Europe which was armed to the teeth, the German Reich was bewildered, a prey to the uncertain, vicissitudinous politics of the Kaiser and his petty advisers. In 1914 there was an assassination in Sarajevo; a misguided, fanatical sixteen-year-old shot the Archduke Francis Ferdinand of Austria and his wife, so unleashing the catastrophe of the Great War on western civilization; Kaiser William attempted to keep the peace by imploring and calling upon the other nations, but at the same time he promised "Nibelung" solidarity with the incensed Austrians.

The English minister Sir Edward

Below: this painting by Gustav
Marx shows William II reviewing
troops on their way to the front.

Grey said, "If Germany is razed to the ground tomorrow, there is not an Englishman who will not be richer for it". Clémenceau spoke for France, saying that there were "twenty million Germans too many in the world". Austria, whose successor to the throne had been murdered by terrorists supported by Serbia, was unyielding this time. The Austrians marched on Serbia. In spite of Germany's requests, the Czar mobilized the Russian troops. The bilateral treaties automatically came into operation: Germany had to come to Austria's aid, which meant war against Russia, but also against Russia's ally, France. The German Empire declared war on Russia and France on 1st and 3rd August 1914. Later on, the world's negotiators at Versailles were to blame the Germans for the war on the basis of these declarations alone. Destiny ran its course.

The 43 years of peace of this Second Reich, later to be known as the "good old days" came to an end, and with them Germany's longest-ever period of peacetime. This dying age was able to boast great cultural achievements, which had come about in spite of the social and other tensions, in spite of the hypocritical profit-seeking of the middle classes, in spite of the worship and adoration of things military, the last fling of aristocratic decadence and the Kaiser's theatrical operetta-life.

In the world of literature the names of Friedrich Hebbel and Otto Ludwig were joined by great newcomers such as Geibel, Heyse, Scheffel, Gustav Freytag, Gottfried Keller, Fritz Reuter, C. F. Meyer, Wilhelm Raabe, Fontane and Anzengruber. In the pic-

Because of his ambitious plans Emperor William II doomed Germany to total isolation. He had to abdicate on November 9 1918.

torial arts the first Naturalists and Impressionists were coming to fame: Menzel, Rethel, Führich and even Franz Marc. The painters Defregger, Lenbach, Leibl, Max Liebermann and Klinger were competing with sculptors such as Hildebrand, Schaper and Schilling.

Architecture was trying out neo-styles, imitating historical forms; Cologne Cathedral and Ulm Minster were completed, and the magnificent Reichstag Building was built in Berlin by Wallot. Germany's enviable musical tradition was carried on by Richard Wagner and Brahms. There is also a long, glowing list of names which distinguished themselves in the sphere of science and invention. In the field of medicine the fame of Virchow, Robert Koch, Bering and Ehrlich spread; Röntgen discovered his X-rays, Pettenkofer founded his doctrine of public hygiene, Einstein had already published the first part of his theory of relativity, and Max Planck revealed his quantum theory. Besides all this, Germany also produced a number of important geographers, explorers, cartographers, historians, philologists, and national economists. There were countless inventions in the technical field: Bauer built the first submarine, Werner von Siemens created a new energy machine—the dynamo, Daimler-Benz produced the automobile and Otto Lilienthal and Count Zeppelin played their part in conquering the skies; the German chemical industry produced aniline and countless new pharmaceutical products and synthetic materials.

This was the aspiring world of a doomed age, an age which was shot to the heart by the assassin at Sarajevo, and which was silenced by the marching of the mobilized armies. This era of thrones and middle classes, of religion and changing values was nearing its end. 1917, the center of the Great War which turned the whole world upside down, marks the beginning of Modern Times.

It was in this year—1917—that the two future World Powers, the USA and the Soviet Union, entered the arena; in this year the socialist revolution under Lenin was successful in Russia, opening up the way for the rise of the proletariat to the ruling classes; in this same year Rutherford paved the way to atomic fission, and Einstein published the second part of his theory of relativity, which made Newton's advances in physics possible. Also in 1917, Oswald Spengler's book, "The Decline of the Western World" was published.

The scene changed rapidly, and when this war of the giants was over, nothing would ever be the same again.

9 From World War to World War

By virtue of its technical expenditure, its massive mobilization, the number of its victims, the amount of destruction and the extent of its battle-fields, the First World War overshadows any other comparable historical event. The German Empire opened the fighting with her famous Schlieffen plan, which involved a massive attack by the right wing of her army across neutral Belgium. This brutal action induced England to enter the war. Germany's rapid sweep through Belgium and northern France, aimed ultimately at Paris, came to a halt at the Battle of the Marne. The front had to turn back, and became fixed from then on in the terrible trench line, the mighty stroke against Verdun, the struggles along the Somme, in the Champagne region and in Flanders. For the first time in history planes and tanks, long-distance guns, gas and flame-throwers were used in the fighting. While the main forces of the German army were concentrated in a desperate effort to

gain a decisive victory in the west, the Russian "steam-roller" with its massive armies, was moving steadily towards the eastern frontiers.

Generals Hindenburg and Ludendorff brought the Russians to a standstill at the Battles of Tannenberg and the Masurian Lakes, went on to encircle them, then succeeded in driving them back deep into the Russian interior. At the most dangerous point of the war, when Germany was sending in her last reserves, her former ally, Italy, then the pro-French Rumanians, attacked her flanks in 1915 and 1916 respectively. In the meantime England was trying to prepare a fatal blow from the Balkan side, seized the straits near the Gallipoli peninsula, seized Turkey, and attacked the south-eastern front with the aid of the Greeks.

By this time nations were fighting each other from the Suez Canal to Flanders, from the Baltic as far as East Africa. There was an encounter between German and British battleships in the Skagerrak in 1916, but since there was no decisive outcome the Germans decided to launch a full-scale submarine war, whilst the British continued their grim hunger-blockade of Germany. Even in the far-distant oceans of the world, battleships were shooting at each other, merchant ships were being sunk, zeppelins were bombing London and the colonial Powers were recruiting colored armies now to fight the Germans: Gurkhas, Sikhs, Chinese, Senegalese and Congolese warriors were brought into the fray. The legend of white man's superiority was destroyed, the colonial Powers themselves taught the Third World how to use automatic weapons and explosives, and spread modern ideas of liberty and democracy. The war of the media was

Bottom of opposite page: on August 1 1914 the German newspapers published the order for general mobilisation; here, the "Berliner Morgenpost" The men who had gone off to the war with flowers in their guns, expecting to be back for Christmas, found that they had to dig in for four grim years of trench warfare. The "war of positions" began.

also raging around the fronts: the press was stirring up the feeling of all humanity against the Germans, calling them Huns and accusing them of all possible atrocities. Dozens of smaller states joined forces with the Western Allies against Germany and her handful of allies, known as the Central Powers. Just as revolution was toppling the Czar's throne in Russia, and German troops were taking advantage of the chaos there to force their way through to St. Petersburg and the Caucasus, the USA declared war on Germany.

All the valor and sacrifice of the nation were in vain: the opposition was now overwhelming in numbers, materials, weapons and aid; the blockade, hunger and exhaustion had taken their toll; General Ludendorff himself had to ask the Kaiser to negotiate a cease-fire. It was too late, however, for in Berlin, in the naval ports and in Munich revolution broke out. The Kaiser was deposed and had to flee to Holland; the Social Democrat Ebert took over power. It was this courageous, honest man who saved Germany from the clutches of the Spartacists and the Communists. The First World War was over, leaving ten million dead, twenty million maimed, and financial losses of around 1,350 billion Goldmarks to the Western World. Europe was a heap of ruins, Germany was in decline, a country torn by revolution, civil war and starvation. In the east the new Soviet world Power was in the making, and

103

the American giant had risen up over the Atlantic. But at first it seemed as though the old Powers of England and France were to determine the fate of the world. At Versailles, and in other Paris suburbs, a peace conference met, which forced Germany to play the role of the accused, completely-defeated, wholly-responsible nation.

In the most humiliating way the Germans were forced to sign an admission of their "war guilt". Substantial border territories were taken from them, for example Eupen-Malmedy, Alsace-Lorraine, Upper Silesia, Posen, West Prussia and parts of Slesvig. Danzig became a "free town" with no rights of access to the Germans: a controversy which, of necessity, was certain to give rise to the next war. When the relinquished border territories, which had been given the freedom to vote, gave a large majority to the pro-German cause, Poland stepped in to intervene, thereby provoking passionate struggles by the "Free-corps" of ex-soldiers. In the

Baltic, too, German troops were still fighting the advancing Bolsheviks.

Under pressure from the Western Allies they all now had to lay down their arms. All Germany's colonies fell to the victors; this nation on the verge of starvation was ordered to hand over 140,000 head of cattle, 30,000 horses and all that remained of her merchant fleet. The German army and navy were destroyed. She was to renounce all military service and reduce her army (Reichswehr) to a hundred thousand regular soldiers, whilst her former enemies were rapidly rearming.

As security for the enormous war reparations demanded from Germany (a bar of gold which would reach half way from the earth to the moon), the left bank of the Rhine was to be occupied for a period of 15 years. When Germany's deliveries of wood and coal fell below to amounts prescribed by the allies, French troops moved into Frankfurt and the Ruhr. The defunct Empire—now a repub-

lic—remained for several years the powerless toy of the victors.

In the meantime the majority-party of Social Democrats under Ebert and Noske had succeeded in quelling the Spartacist revolution, the communist uprisings and the national strikes. On 19th January 1919 the National Assembly met in Weimar and began to draw up a republican constitution. This "Weimar Republic" (1919–1933) was to last for fourteen years.

This young republic took on the terrible burden of the lost war, the impossible debt in war reparations, which would need three generations to repay. This new government, supported only by the immense patience and incomparable energy of the working populace, had to set about restoring the destroyed, dismantled, out-moded factories and relieving the grave threat of starvation. The draining of all her gold reserves, the huge national debt, and above all, the occupation of the Ruhr with its industry and coal resources, brought on galloping inflation. Very soon a loaf of bread cost millions of Reichsmarks and tram fares were half a billion marks. The middle classes lost their savings and, faced by the greatest hardships, were forced to throw away their property. A new race of black-marketeers and racketeers emerged.

Many officers and soldiers of the disbanded armies were not able to grasp, after all they had gone through, after all the sacrifice, the heroic deeds and the initial victories, that the war had indeed been lost. The "stab-in-the-back" legend was born, the myth grew of betrayal by the Social Democrats or by the Jews. The humiliated German national feeling, trampled and crippled by the Treaty of Versailles, re-awoke too late, then developed too fanatically into vehement nationalism. The harshness of Versailles, the continuing humiliation by the victorious powers, the occupation of the Rhineland, the persistent encroachment on the eastern borders by Polish volunteers, the way in which Germany was treated as a colonial territory, the desperate poverty, unemployment and the latent threat of Communism all created a climate for "Free-corps", militant groups such as the "steel helmets", vehmic groups and national youth movements; but most dangerous of all, this climate was also ideal for the growth of radical rightwing parties. A demagogue by the name of Adolf Hitler had already founded in Munich his NSDAP, which was backed up by military movements such as the SA and SS; he had joined up with the Free-corps, the *Reichswehr* and militant Bavarian groups to prepare for his *putsch* against the Social Democratic government in 1923. This first amateurish attempt failed, but this new movement was not wiped

out. When Hitler came out of his short imprisonment he began his political activity in earnest and created a Fascist party which grew at an amazing rate because of the increasing poverty, the growing threat from the "red front", from the Spartacist movement and from other radical left-wing groups; Hitler's party itself now grew into a danger for the Republic.

The short-lived history of the Weimar Republic, with all its honest attempts at reconstruction, the creation of order, freedom and the assurance of a future for the nation, ended in the catastrophe of unchained, uncontrolled nationalism.

The short-sighted victor-nations only added fuel to Hitler's fire: the Germans were working like slaves for nothing, since all the hard-earned results of their production disappeared abroad as war reparations, only to create new problems by crippling and destroying the economies of the nations concerned; the world economic crisis, the Great Depression was inevitable in view of all this. Governments

came and went in the endless party squabbles among the 36 German political parties; the newspapers uncovered more and more corruption scandals, such as Barmat, Kutisker and Sklarek. Adolf Hitler persuaded the poor exploited masses of poverty-stricken proletarians that the Jews and the "reds" were to blame for everything, and that Germany's only hope was to achieve equal status once more by strengthening her defenses and ridding herself of alien elements—by becoming truly and genuinely German again. In this seemingly hopeless situation, more and more Germans believed in this new "Messiah". In 1932 Hitler's NSDAP gained twelve million votes and the Communist Party had five million. The combined democratic parties were left with only eighteen and a half million. The bank crisis set in and the unemployment figures rose to almost seven million. A delay for payment of the reparations bill was granted and some relief for Germany was accorded by the Allies, but by this time it was all too late. The

bricks and mortar of Germany's cities were already trembling at the marching goose-step of Hitler's brown-uniformed followers; every Sunday saw dozens of dead left on the streets after delirious party rallies.

When Brüning's government, along with the re-elected President Hindenburg, were only able to govern by the use of "emergency measures", as the socialist parties were joining to form the "iron front", and the moderate nationalists were uniting with the Fascists to form the "Harzburg front", as the uniforms of the SA, SS, red front, steel helmets, Bavarian guard and other movements were parading the streets, the frightened middle classes were shocked into thinking that there was only one choice left open to them: the choice between the blood-red Communists and Hitler's brown uniforms.

The horrific reports of the Russian Revolution and the cruel Communist rebellions were still fresh in German memories, whereas Hitler promised *"Arbeit und Brot"* (work and bread),

At the end of the war the opposing forces within the defeated Reich clashed violently. In some regions of Germany, such as Thuringia and Munich, workers' revolutions led to the creation of the "Republic of Councils". The movement was savagely repressed.

Friedrich Ebert (1871–1925) and his moderate party (SPD) restored order and enabled the German economy to recover.

freedom and a glorious future; the majority of the middle classes moved therefore towards the "Third Reich" which was now in the making.

The German Republic was granted only a short space of time in which to form itself: it had fourteen turbulent years of arbitrary occupation by foreign powers, struggles by separatist movements, communist and nationalist rebellions, inflation, economic crisis, a bank crash, corruption, endless, futile international conferences and a powerless League of Nations, yet in all this there were a few bright sparks which could have brought hope to the German nation.

As early as 17th April 1922 the German Foreign Minister, Rathenau, had succeeded in forming a special pact with the Soviet Union, promising mutual aid for the two nations. Soon after, however, Rathenau was assassinated, Russia allowed the Germans secretly to build up a forbidden stock of weapons such as tanks and air force materials, which were stored on Soviet soil.

There was, however, no real co-operation between the great nations. Another glimmer of hope lay in the "Geneva Convention for the Peaceful Settlement of International Disputes" (1924), which failed, however, due to England's refusal to sign. At the Conference of Locarno in 1925, an agreement was reached between the German minister Stresemann and his French partner, Aristide Briand. They undertook to respect the existing frontiers, to keep the peace, and the evacuation of the Rhineland was promised. As a result of this agreement Germany was finally admitted to the League of Nations on 8th September 1926. Unfortunately, Stresemann died soon after and Briand lost his power in his own country. The "spirit of Locarno" was not fulfilled and Adolf Hitler wiped it out completely.

Towards the end of the Weimar Republic, Germany's political skies appeared to be clearing a little: a conference in The Hague submitted the Young Plan, which eased the pressure

on Germany in respect of reparation payments, and set an ultimatum for the evacuation of the Rhineland (1930). The Kellogg Pact of 1928 and a whole series of disarmament conferences seemed to be aiming at world peace. At the same time, however, at the instigation of Russia in the east and France in the west, a whole complex of bilateral, or even multilateral pacts was beginning to entangle Europe, pacts which Adolf Hitler construed as being directed against Germany. During the world economic crisis it finally came to the Hoover Moratorium which postponed Germany's deadline for payment; the Lausanne Conference of 1932 had already decreed that Germany was now only to pay three billion gold marks on top of the 53.1 billion she had already paid; (the original sum demanded had been 285 billion).

The crisis was already drawing to its close, as was the era of the Weimar Republic, when the internal political conflict between Germany's parties plunged the country into the hasty

George Grosz called his painting, (opposite page) "The Pillars of Society". In it, he caricaturises the society of the Weimar Republic in which he saw militarists, petty bourgeois, corrupt judges and hypocritical pacifists.

consequences of the 1932 electoral battle. Hitler's party now proved to be the strongest in the *Reichstag*, but was still a long way from having an absolute majority. General Streicher made a last attempt to unite the trade unions and the Socialist wing of the NSDAP under the leadership of Gregor Strasser, in order to prevent Hitler's seizing power over the country; this attempt failed, not least because of the aged President Hindenburg who had fallen out with the Socialists over his subventions to landowners east of the Elbe *(Osthilfe)* and who believed that he could prevent a left-wing *putsch* only by appointing Hitler. For Hitler brought with him the support of the German nationalists, the "steel-helmets", the Conservatives and the powers of capitalism. Therefore, on 30th January 1933 Hindenburg handed over the reins of government to this man from Braunau.

Even the least fanatical followers and opponents of Hitler had read his cruel and confused book "Mein Kampf"; many of them had not taken very seriously his expression of his hatred of Jews and Socialists, believing it to be nothing more than the intoxicated outpourings of an era which was loaded with political jargon. Almost all of these people believed that this Chancellor appointed by the President would govern the country according to the constitution, abide by its laws and fulfil his promises of work and food, liberty, equality and prosperity. The nation was relieved that the bloody political conflict between their parties was now over. They soon learned, however, to recognize the true face of National Socialism. On 27th February 1933 the *Reichstag* building was burned down: this provided Hitler with an excuse for the rapid persecution of the Communists.

The economic crisis hit Germany hard. In 1924, galloping inflation was held in check. But the autumn of 1928 marked the beginning of the end for the country's modest economic recovery. Soon there were two million unemployed, and the number kept on rising until March 1932, when it exceeded six million.

The whole of the Social Democratic press was silenced. The parliamentary elections of 5th March 1933 brought Hitler's party, combined with the Conservative front, "black-white-red" a narrow majority with 52% of the votes. Dr. Goebbels became propaganda minister. On 24th March the *Reichstag*, which was by this time terror-struck, passed the "Enabling Act" *(Ermächtigungsgesetz)*, which gave Hitler absolute, dictatorial power.

He immediately brought every one of the former states *(Länder)* under centralized control by appointing governors *(Reichsstatthalter)* to each one; he abolished the trade unions and forced all political parties other than his own to disband. The next parliamentary elections in November brought Hitler's NSDAP and their

associates 92% of all votes. The dictatorship was well and truly established, all civil liberty disappeared and the history of Germany ran its inevitable course.

In this totalitarian state all aspects of life were "co-ordinated" *(gleichgeschaltet)*; the workers had to join the German Workers' Front, farmers had to join the Food Estate (Reichsnährstand), whilst all writers who were not able or willing to emigrate had to join the Reich's Chamber of Culture *(Reichsschrifttumskammer)*; children were enlisted into the Hitler Youth or the German Girls' Movement, the women into the women's league, the men into the SA, SS, the Drivers' Corps or the Flying Squad: there was no association or professional body, no official position, newspaper or commercial enterprise which was not brought into the almighty party-line. A secret state police (Gestapo) and a security service (SD) were set up under Heinrich Himmler's control; concentration camps were built for all political, religious or "racial" opponents—these were hidden away across the moors and beyond the forests, surrounded by sentries and barbed wire, so that the nation could not learn the truth about what was going on.

Only the army (the *Reichswehr*) did not fall so easily into the hands of the Nazi system. The President remained its Supreme Commander and most of the officers' corps regarded Hitler with suspicion and dislike. When Ernst Röhm, supported by the gigantic SA army, supposedly revolted, hoping to establish a Socialist military corps, based on a newly-formed version of the SA, Hitler seized the opportunity of wiping out all his opponents. He had Röhm and his close supporters shot without trial, but also

from that date on (30th June 1934) he systematically sought out and executed all former political opponents, as well as his former accomplices and all people who had known him beforehand and would have been able to give adverse reports of him.

Once the Jewish pogrom was underway the German nation had to face the truth and realize just whom they had elected to power; but, by this time, Hitler had become a law unto himself, and no-one could touch him. For now the generals were also gathering around him; they even accepted it when General Schleicher was shot. These generals were now obtaining their full re-armament, soon general national service was re-introduced, then came the naval pact with England and the military occupation of the Rhineland. On 25th June 1934 the

Below, left: Aristide Briand and Gustav Stresemann were committed to better relations between France and Germany. Below, right: this handshake between Hitler and Hindenburg, on March 1933, symbolized the "union of the old and the new".

halt, the right to re-arm was made official. No nation moved against Hitler's occupation of the demilitarized Rhineland zone, or against his breach of the Locarno Pact; they accepted his re-introduction of conscription; the Churches made concordats with this violent leader and statesmen visited him at his mountain retreat—men such as Lloyd George, the Prince of Wales, Neville Chamberlain and Daladier. Some of them, after their visit, even used the familiar greeting "Heil Hitler", because his magnetic personality had bewitched them.

In 1936 the world was Germany's guest at the spectacular Olympic Games in Berlin. The great sporting event turned into a great tribute to Adolf Hitler; the Soviet Union was alone in declining to take part.

ancient President Hindenburg finally died and Hitler proclaimed himself both President and Chancellor, calling himself *Führer* (leader). The armed forces immediately came under his supreme command, and had to swear an oath of allegiance.

It became more and more evident that this dictator's crazy ideas, racial hatred, deadly enmity of the Socialists and his ideal of marching straight into a new military adventure, were all serious realities to him. But in Germany there was no-one left who could stop him. In 1935 at the Nuremberg Rally he made public his racial laws. From now on proof of "Aryan descent" was a prerequisite to the holding of any official position. The Party governed all aspects of life.

A flood of indoctrination and propaganda overwhelmed the nation. Tens of thousands of teachers and professors hammered home the new ideals with both conviction and inspiration into the hearts of the nation's youth. Large sections of the population looked on in admiration at the Führer's success in regenerating and invigorating the nation, which was suddenly finding a new prosperity. Resistance was limited to small groups of ideological intellectuals, or the few remaining idealistic men and women who were able to see all the suffering, lies and emptiness on which the outward glamor and show of the new system was based.

The problem of unemployment was solved with one great blow. The unemployed were sent to build the autobahns, barracks, new munitions factories, dockyards, ships, planes and arms; new housing estates, recreation centres, theaters and museums appeared. Everything which the surrounding nations had refused to the Weimar Republic, or had only granted reluctantly, they now conceded in the face of Hitler's harsh demands and persistent threats: the payment of reparations remained at a

Below, right: drawing by George Grosz denouncing the Reichswehr, which did not hesitate to become the instrument of Hitler's war plans.
Bottom: Hitler and Mussolini concluded the "Rome–Berlin Axis" in 1936; this was a treaty of alliance which they completed in 1939 with the "Pact of Steel".

In 1934 Adolf Hitler—the son of a petty customs official, a corporal of the First World War, a casual laborer and beerhouse painter—had made his first journey abroad to meet Mussolini in Venice. The German Fascist had met the inventor of Fascism.

After an initial rivalry over the Austrian question, the two dictators came to an arrangement. When Mussolini attacked and conquered the peaceful African nation of Abyssinia (Ethiopia), the League of Nations isolated him and imposed sanctions on Italy; Hitler's hour had come—he delivered coal, oil and weapons to Mussolini and saved his "Imperium" for him. In return he was given the go-ahead by the Duce for his long-desired annexation of Austria.

As early as 1934 Hitler had engi-neered a *putsch* in Vienna, but had failed. By 1938 the Third Reich was strong and powerful enough to carry through its plans and set right the last great mistake of the hated Treaty of Versailles.

In 1936 Hitler had already re-established Germany's sovereignty over her great rivers. In 1937 Mussolini made a triumphal visit to Germany and the two dictators laid the foundations of their subsequent "Axis alliance", based on the theory that the vertical axis of Europe passed through Rome and Berlin. This "Axis" had once been the heart of the Holy German Empire.

Early in 1938, Austria was troubled by internal political conflicts, as a strong National Socialist party had grown up there. On 13th March of the

same year Hitler marched into Austria. With flowers, tears and great rejoicing the two German states were re-united. The thousand years of common history brought them back together, and all memory of Bismarck's "Lesser Germany" solution was extinguished, along with the Versailles Treaty's condition that Austria should never again be annexed to Germany.

Such historic events stunned the growing number of critics of Hitler's politics and of his persistent breaches of the law. They hardly noticed Colonel General Beck's resignation, the dismissal of Schacht, the minister for economic affairs, and the departure of the minister for foreign affairs, Neurath. Even Colonel General Fritsch,

who had a reserved attitude towards Hitler's obvious war-policy, was shamefully discharged.

Hitler, however, was already offering the public his next, unbelievable successes. After the annexation of Austria he had unleashed the question of the Sudeten Germans. The Treaty of Versailles had delivered 3$\frac{1}{2}$ million German-speaking Sudetens to Czechoslovakia. Hitler resolved to annex them to Germany and correct this wrong.

Yet again Hitler's method of diplomacy by massive threats paid off: Daladier, Chamberlain and Mussolini met him in Munich. The Munich Agreement surrendered these Czech border-lands to Germany and the Sudetens became geographically,

economically and politically dependent on Hitler. When Chamberlain returned to London he triumphantly waved the piece of paper on which Hitler had undertaken that "there would be no war in this nor the next generation".

No-one in Europe wanted war, but not everyone believed by this time that war could be avoided. More hard-line politicians were entering the scene—such as Churchill in England and Mendès in France. Hitler very soon gave them proof that they could not live with him in peace. On 9th November 1938 Dr. Goebbels, on Hitler's orders, stirred up ugly riots against the Jews, thereby outraging the whole of the cultured world. In March 1939 Hitler's army marched into the

rest of Czechoslovakia and occupied Prague without meeting with any resistance. With this action Hitler had stepped over the line which separated the justifiable from the downright criminal. As Churchill said at the time: "Only a fool takes what he already owns!"

Hitler had finally broken all international trust. When German troops marched in to occupy the Memel territory on 25th March 1939, Chamberlain announced in his speech at Birmingham that the end of appeasement had come. From now on they were going to get tough with Hitler.

In spite of this threatening sign, Hitler took up the Polish question: he wanted the return of the Danzig corridor to Germany and free autobahn access to the east. These demands came at the wrong time and met with a prompt and blunt refusal. Chamberlain pledged Anglo-French support to the Poles in case of an attack on their territory.

Events were coming to a head. Pacts of mutual military assistance were made: there was the "Pact of Steel" between Germany and Italy, the British guarantees for Greece, Turkey, and Rumania and the renewal of the Franco-British alliance.

Then came the great bombshell: on 23rd August 1939 Hitler succeeded in negotiating a non-aggression pact with his red dictator-colleague, Stalin; there was a "secret protocol" which provided for the partition of Eastern Europe between the two Powers.

With such an agreement behind him, Hitler believed that he had by now sufficiently intimidated the Western Powers, and that the USA was in an economically and militarily weak position. He used primitive methods to engineer a so-called attack by Polish volunteers on a German transmission post near the border; this incident was used as an excuse to declare war, and Hitler moved his highly-mechanized army into Poland. To his astonishment England and France immediately retaliated by declaring war on Germany; his chief interpreter, Dr. Paul Schmitt, reported that the amazed Führer could say nothing more than *Was nun?* (what now?) when he heard this news.

The Second World War had begun.

10 Hitlers War and its Consequences

The German army had been newly built up and was equipped with all modern aids, highly mechanized and motorized, and far outnumbered the others. It began the war with a series of "Blitzkriegs" which enabled Hitler's forces to defeat and occupy Poland in eighteen days, Holland, Belgium and France in six weeks, Denmark and Norway in three weeks. Within three weeks England was swept away from the Continent; then German power defeated Yugoslavia in three weeks, Greece and Crete were taken in a further seven weeks, making Germany the ruler over Europe.

The German nation was not enticed into this Second World War with flowers, flags and laurel-wreaths; there was no rejoicing or great zeal. The people rose up in all earnestness, and even the army itself was well

aware that it was sent out to solve a hard, basically insoluble problem. The memories of Verdun, of the mud-battles of the First World War, of its suffering, starvation and final defeat, were still fresh in their memories. They suspected too, that the re-arming and preparation for the war were far too hasty and amateurish, although no-one fully realized that Hitler, in his impatience, had failed to make use of the great new discoveries and inventions, and that these would not be available for the coming fateful struggle; in 1936 Otto Hahn and Lise Meitner had successfully carried out atomic fission, in 1934 Messerschmitt had invented the jet-plane, the use of radar had been perfected since 1931, and plans for long-distance rockets had been available since 1932. Even the air-force, on Hitler's orders, had been developed along the wrong lines,

so that the *Luftwaffe* expert in charge of air operations shot himself.

Hitler entered upon this great war in an irresponsible, improvising manner. At first the news flashes and fanfare-reports of speedy victories, U-boat successes, air-battles and the occupation of foreign countries all served to arouse the reluctant enthusiasm of the nation. Italy and a few small Balkan states entered the war on Germany's side, and soon the war was raging in North Africa and the Near East. Then, however, in the fall of 1940, came the defeat in the Battle of Britain—the series of quick, easy occupations of foreign territory seemed to have come to a halt. When he awoke from his intoxication after the victories of his *Blitzkrieg*, Hitler was faced with the same situation as had previously frustrated Napoleon. Both men had been able to occupy Europe through the use of their superior military machine—but both had been halted by the resistance of the British Isles, which prevented the final victory.

Thus Hitler and his German Reich had to follow the same fateful paths as Napoleon and the French Empire. Geography, economy and politics had all pre-destined his strategy. There were four possibilities for defeating England. He could try invasion tactics, but this required a superior navy and absolute supremacy in the air. It was England who possessed the superior fleet, and she soon had an equally powerful air-force. Was it possible to bring England to her knees by means of an economic and food blockade? Napoleon had tried it with his Continental Blockade. Hitler decided on a radical submarine attack on the British navy, and sent out his bombers over the oceans. However, radar and massive aid from the USA prevented

his fatal stranglehold. Soon the German U-boats were hunted out like wild animals.

A third possibility led both Napoleon and Hitler in the direction of Egypt and the Middle East, in an attempt to bring about the collapse of the British Empire and her central Indian bastion. The heroic struggle of the German *Afrika Korps* under Rommel failed through Hitler's erroneous decisions, a lack of reinforcements, inferior naval and air command, coupled with the weakness of the Italians. The German surrender of Tunis in 1942 was a decisive event of the war. Hitler's lust for power, and his sheer stupidity had led him to make a tragic decision. He followed Napoleon's fourth way, seeking to attack England by defeating Russia; he attacked the Soviet Union and concentrated the strength of his *Wehrmacht* in the East.

The Germans found Stalin's armies unprepared. They marched into a country which did not want war and was poorly prepared for it. Once again the German propaganda machines were able to report massive battles of encirclement, great victories and unimpeded advances. Even at this point Hitler, who had meanwhile appointed himself commander-in-chief of the army, made more fatal decisions. In the middle of the assault on Moscow, he sent the army on a six-week campaign in the Ukraine; he changed the image of his army from one of "liberator from the yoke of Communism" to one of "angel of death and revenge"; he sent his party-bosses into the occupied provinces, where they behaved like tyrants, stirring up mass-murders, kidnappings, looting and other outrages, until they finally brought about the "Winter War" in Russia.

In the winter of 1941, as the Sibe-

rian relief army advanced, and the German army, which was not equipped for a winter offensive, was stuck in the snow and ice, came the retreat from Moscow. After the last desperate advance in 1942, aimed at the Volga and Caucasus, followed the Stalingrad catastrophe. At the beginning of 1943, the surrounded city fell and the German Sixth Army died, betrayed by Hitler and Goering. From then on, the tide turned for Germany; all the courage, strength and sacrifice of the German people was bled dry in a series of battles of retreat.

Meanwhile Hitler's megalomania had provoked him to declare war on the USA, so that half the world—72 states of the earth—were united against Nazi Germany. There were mountains of materials and military reinforcements stacked against her, whilst Germany suffered continuous bomb attacks and her ancient cities,

her industrial zones, her arsenals, docks and factories all lay in ruins and sank into rubble and ashes.

War had gripped the whole surface of the earth. On the seas, in the air, in deserts, jungles, steppes and in the ancient cultural landscapes of history, gigantic armies were waging great battles of technology; the USA continued to pump in an endless stream of weapons, machines, ships, engines and oil. Germany's heavily-populated cultural and industrial areas sank into ruin under the prolonged, unceasing bomb attacks. The people who had patiently undertaken the torment and suffering of the hopeless campaigns, now breathed their last and died silently in the ruins of their homeland.

Since the war had become cruel and hard for Germany, Hitler and his party chiefs dropped all pretences and stopped playing at abiding by the rules of morality, humanity and Christian-

In a few weeks the German divisions swept aside the Soviet positions and by October 1941 had come within a few miles of Moscow. The Soviet counter-offensive did not begin until November 1942. The German defeat at Stalingrad (below), on February 2 1943, marked a decisive turning-point in the course of the war.

ity; their infernal hatred became horrific action. They hoped to achieve a "Final Solution to the Jewish question". The Jews in occupied Europe were rounded up by force and transported to the east, where German SS commandos had for some time now been filling mass graves with the bodies of exterminated Jews. The chimneys of the concentration camps

Hitler's system swept away the German nation's thousand years of history, a history which, compared to belched out smoke and the gas-chambers worked non-stop; there were orgies of mass murder on whole races. other nations' histories, was comparatively free from outrage and mass murder; he created an indelible stigma which was later revealed in the

piles of corpses and the bone-pits of the hundreds of concentration camps. Only a fraction of Germany's population knew anything of these monstrosities, but they would all have to bear the consequences of them later.

Then the world's revenge rose up out of the sea: Americans and Britons landed on the Normandy coast in the summer of 1944, broke through the Atlantic Wall and advanced into German territory.

Resistance from inside Germany arose in vain and too late. A group of officers attempted the revolt of 20th July 1944, but failed to undermine Hitler's "perfect system"; they were executed after a hasty judgement by the People's Court (*Volksgerichtshof*). Armies broke through the German frontiers from the east and the west. The death-struggle of a great nation still demanded enormous sacrifice of life; Hitler finally shot himself in the bunker of his destroyed Chancellery in Berlin. The Soviets had already hoisted their blood-red flag over the Reichstag building. The Americans were on the Elbe. The end had arrived in terror and the Third Reich collapsed into shreds. On 8th May 1945 the *Wehrmacht* capitulated. At the Yalta Conference the leaders of the victorious nations had already decided upon the division of Germany between them, and the shape of the zones of post-war Germany was now outlined. America, Russia, England and France divided up the German territory. The Americans, by giving up Thuringia and parts of Saxony and Brandenburg, paid for the right to be one of the occupying powers in Berlin. And they forgot to take the precaution of arranging an assured right of access to the city from the west. From now on Berlin became an island in an ocean of Soviet administration.

British and American air raids against enemy military targets began in 1942 and went on daily from 1943, devastating large numbers of German cities.

At the Potsdam Conference the Allies decreed that "all German authorities, administrative bodies and the German people were to comply unconditionally with the demands of the Allies".

These were the consequences of the "unconditional surrender" which had been heralded as early as 1942 in Casablanca. The end of the war meant the loss of all territories, all oases of German culture, all the settlements and distant outposts which the nation had created for itself in more than eight hundred years of her history. Provinces such as East and West Prussia, Silesia, German settlement areas such as the Sudetenland, Moravia, Bohemia, the Banat and the Batschka were not only annexed, but were emptied of their German population. About fourteen million refugees, harassed and exploited, streamed towards the shrunken territory of rubble heaps which was now Germany. It was only now that this great nation in the heart of Europe truly became the *"Volk ohne Raum"* (people without living-space) which Hitler had made speeches about. This remnant of Germany, at the end of Hitler's twelve-year folly, was left with a national debt estimated by Eisenhower at around four hundred billion Marks. The majority of her cities were more than 50% destroyed, her industrial premises were bombed out, and what remained of her mechanical equipment was soon dismantled. German patents and inventions now became the property of her conquerors; her art treasures were removed from their museums and disappeared abroad, where they remained as payment for damaged or destroyed valuables in the other countries. Her entire gold reserves, her foreign capital, ships and all transportable industrial installations were seized by the victors.

Hunger and homelessness prevailed throughout Germany. Hundreds of thousands of foreign workers were passing through, sometimes robbing, burning and raping their way through the provinces. Occupation troops had to be sent in to maintain order.

At first the daily food ration of a German person consisted of 1150 calories. Robbery and black-marketeering were the order of the day.

The Allied Powers soon stated their claims for war reparations. The Soviet Union at first demanded ten billion US dollars; Byrne, the American Secretary of State; declared, however, that "from East Prussia and Silesia alone, the USSR had obtained fourteen billion dollars' worth of reparations." Meanwhile the whole German population underwent a "denazification" process. This meant that every man and every woman was checked out for their attitude towards Hitler and his system, and retrospective laws allowed them to be punished according to the degree of their participation in the former state.

The Nuremberg Trials were set in

117

Facing: instead of surrendering, the Nazis did not hesitate to recruit children of 12 or 13 during the final phase of the war.

motion to try the big Party leaders and those responsible for this world-wide catastrophe; a series of smaller proceedings followed on from these. High officials of the state, German generals and members of the middle ranks of the Party waited in dozens of prison camps.

When the Allied troops had marched into German territory and freed the first concentration camps, their shock at the unspeakable horrors which they found overcame them. For this reason there was a "no fraternization" order for the troops at the beginning of the occupation period.

In spite of this order, it was largely the Americans, with their "care packages", their Red Cross deliveries and the personal help of the occupying soldiers, who aided the Germans through the first post-war winter and gave them the chance of survival.

World opinion was still outraged and contradictory. The world press and continuous radio broadcasts transmitted the message of hatred, the "collective guilt of all Germans". For years it seemed as if no German would ever again be able to venture across the frontiers of his country, which was "destined for sheep-grazing land"; it seemed as if the Germans were banished for eternity from the community of nations. Even in German history, however, there is no such thing as eternity. Soon there was growing tension between the eastern and western occupying powers. The Americans loosened their stranglehold on Germany and decided to give her a new, fair start.

In 1946 the Double Zone Agreement was reached with Britain. The Double Zone participated in the Marshall Plan and received American economic aid. A national bank, the *"Bank deutscher Länder"* was founded in 1948, and in June of that year there followed the currency reform. A healthy new unit of currency was introduced, the Deutschmark.

The Soviets did not take part in these measures aimed at economic equilibrium, and tried hard to take over complete power in Berlin, which lay within their zone of occupation. The British and Americans responded to this with their massive air-lift, which lasted until May 1949 and saved Berlin from sinking into the red-Communist sea.

On 23rd May 1949, after ratification by the *Landtage* in the west, the

constitution of the Federal Republic of Germany *(Bundesrepublik Deutschland)* was proclaimed; the *Bundestag* and the *Bundesrat* moved into action. Konrad Adenauer was elected first Federal Chancellor and Theodor Heuss the first Federal President.

This new constitution for the new state was the best and most liberal that Germany had ever had. The state was to have a federal construction, pledged to respect social interests, civil liberties and the law. One week later the People's Congress in the Soviet zone confirmed the constitution of the German Democratic Republic *(Deutsche Demokratische Republik).* This completed the division of Ger-

Bottom of opposite page: after the foundation of the Federal Republic of Germany in the Western zones, the German Democratic Republic was set up on October 7 1949 in the Soviet occupation zone. The separation of Germany is most keenly noticeable in Berlin.

Below, right: Willy Brandt became Federal Chancellor in October 1969. In 1971 he received the Nobel Peace Prize for his realistic "Ostpolitik".

many into FRG and GDR. According to the political and ideological system of their occupiers, the Germans had opted for two fundamentally different reforms of their society and state.

In the east Wilhelm Pieck was elected president and Otto Grotewohl became Prime Minister; the People's Chamber of four hundred delegates was still divided into several parties. It was only later that the SED (National Front) party emerged under Walther Ulbricht's leadership as the bearer of the one-party system. Once the new German states had been founded, the reconstruction program took on immense proportions.

Under the rubble of the devastated German Reich something of the indestructible German national spirit survived. These people had become paupers; they were bombed-out, half-starved pariahs without sufficient aid; treated as scapegoats by the whole world, the Germans, immediately after their defeat, rolled up their shirt-sleeves and began to work again. Women worked among the rubble to salvage bricks, old men carted away the rubbish from the cities and children worked in the fields. For millions of German soldiers remained still in the forced labor camps of their victors—especially in the East.

Just as after the Thirty Years' War, the all-important resources of the workers, middle-classes, intellectuals and entrepreneurs were patience, industriousness and inventiveness.

Reconstruction began, and in a few years grew into Germany's astonishing "economic miracle". Economic aid from the Americans at the outset speeded up the process. Tremendous achievements were made in the East and in the West, so that in the sixties the Federal Republic was rated third, and the Democratic Republic achieved fifth place in the ranks of the industrial nations of the world.

At the same time, however, it was again proved, just as after the Thirty Years' War, that the Germans, both in victory and in defeat, have a tendency to immoderation, trying too hard to be the exemplary pupils of the system imposed on them. In the West, the FRG conformed more and more to the American life-style, with its capitalistic, super-democratic behavior; there followed the use of the English language and American slang, with jazz, beat, pop and the hippie-movement becoming more and more popular; then came the drug-addiction, pornography, "liberation from the old values and taboos", the undermining of all authority, and weakness in the state's leadership. Whilst all this was happening in the West, East Germany developed along totally different lines; under Russian occupation, the GDR had a much harder time of it than the FRG: society developed along Socialist lines with strong Communist tendencies, the authority of the State had a strong, dominating influence; the cultural tendency was more towards Russia, and the East German citizen tried hard to be the model Soviet citizen.

The cleft between the two parts of the nation deepened. The Hallstein Doctrine, announced in the West, excluded the possibility of continued diplomatic relations between the

such plan, the Federal Republic finally joined the NATO alliance in 1955.

This, of course, meant a further widening of the gap between the Eastern and Western blocs, and therefore also between East and West Germany. 1957 finally saw the founding of the Common Market, the European Economic Community of France, Italy, the Benelux states and West Germany. The new Germany was striding forth in strength—and, initially, with enthusiasm, towards a united Europe. The remains of the former Empire looked with hope towards a united Europe, working together in a fraternal federation, and saw in this the final fulfilment of the task which the ancient Roman Empire had taken on, and which the medieval Emperors had never been able to complete; the "Empire" was Europe.

However, all this came to nothing in 1961, when the cruellest consequence of the Second World War emerged to divide both Germany and Europe: the Iron Curtain. The division of the nation by the random cease-fire line of 1945 slowly became a real frontier, a particularly hard frontier. Thousands of Germans fled

FRG and countries which had relations with the GDR; this served to harden the situation. The re-establishment of full sovereignty was very much speeded up in West-Germany by the outbreak of the Korean War in 1950; the USA bound itself more closely to Europe and its newly-founded NATO (1949); they also wished to install West-German defences as part of an integrated European defence system. In 1950 the Federal Government in Bonn was invited to join the Council of Europe. Chancellor Adenauer took up the Schuman Plan, and the question of a united Europe was raised. At the same time the great debate over re-militarization began in the FRG. After the Four Powers Conference of 1954, held in Berlin, had failed to make any progress in the direction of re-unification of the German nation, on account of Soviet resistance to any across this line on the map, which divided the one-party state from the free-market economy with its higher living-standards. The GDR was being drained of its artisans, experts and work-force, which it could ill afford in its hard program of work.

Thus came the building of the Wall straight through Berlin; mine-fields, barbed-wire fences and electric alarm systems were laid along the former border between the occupation zones. From now on the border sentries shot at fellow German citizens who tried to flee from one part of Germany to another. The Hallstein Doctrine could alter nothing in the stubborn attitude of the East.

And so it came to Socialist Federal Chancellor Brandt's controversial "Ostpolitik", which breached the Hallstein Doctrine and sought to establish tolerable diplomatic relations with certain states in the eastern bloc.

As a result of this Eastern policy both the FRG and the GDR were finally accorded full-member status of the United Nations Organization in 1973. This, of course, did nothing to remove the division between the two parts of the nation, nor even to improve their situation to any great extent.

The Federal Republic still belongs to NATO and the EEC, whilst East Germany is a member of the Warsaw Military Pact and of the eastern Council for Mutual Economic Assistance.

Thus the two Germanies, one of which has recently solemnly declared that it no longer belongs to the German nation, go their own ways towards a new age—as great economic powers, but political satellites of the future. The German "Reich" is nothing but history.

Chronology

719	Saint Boniface begins to evangelize Germania.
732	Charles Martel defeats the Arabs at Poitiers.
742	The *Concilium Germanicum* is convened by Saint Boniface.
751	Pippin the Short is crowned King of the Franks at Soissons.
768	Death of Pippin the Short.
771	Charlemagne, sole King of the Franks.
782–785	Conquest of Saxony by Charlemagne.
800	Charlemagne is crowned Emperor.
806	Submission of the Sorabians.
814	Death of Charlemagne.
830	Louis the Pious is dethroned by his sons.
842	Oaths of Strasbourg.
843	Treaty of Verdun.
891	Battle against the Normans on the Dyle.
911	Conrad I of Franconia is elected King of Germania.
925	Lorraine becomes a Germanic duchy.
919–936	Reign of Henry I (in 955, victory over the Hungarians at the Unstrut).
936–973	Otto I the Great.
955	Victory over the Hungarians at Augsburg.
962	Otto I is crowned Emperor.
1014	Henry II crowned Emperor.
1033	Burgundy joined to Germany.
1046	Henry III crowned Emperor.
1055	Henry III's second Italian campaign.
1062	Henry IV kidnapped while still a minor.
1077	Henry IV humiliated at Canossa.
1084	Henry IV is crowned Emperor.
1096–1099	First Crusade.
1106	On the death of Henry IV, Henry V ascends the throne.
1122	The Concordat of Worms puts an end to the quarrel over the Investitures.
1138–1152	Reign of Conrad III.
1152–1190	Frederick I.
1154–1159	First expedition against Italy—Barbarossa is crowned Emperor.
1158–1162	Barbarossa's second Italian campaign.
1163–1178	More raids by Barbarossa into Italy.
1176	Defeat at Legnano.
1177	Peace Treaty of Venice.
1180	Henry the Lion is banished from the Empire.
1184	Whitsun at Mainz.
1189	Crusade of Frederick Barbarossa, who dies in 1190.
1190–1197	Henry VI Emperor.
1198	Election of two successors to Henry VI.
1202–1204	Fourth Crusade.
1212–1250	Frederick II of Hohenstaufen.
1214	Battle of Bouvines.
1220	Frederick II crowned Emperor.
1234	The Steding peasant revolt is crushed.
1236	The beginning of conflict with the Lombards and the Holy See.
1241	The German knights routed by the Mongols at Legnica.
1250	Death of Frederick II.
1254	Death of Conrad IV.
1256	Beginning of the Great Interregnum.
1267	Italian campaign of the young Conrad V, or Conradin, who was beheaded in 1268.
1273–1291	The cantons of Schwyz, Uri and Unterwald sign the perpetual Pact.
1298	The elective Germanic crown goes to Albert of Austria.
1308–1313	... then to Henry of Luxembourg
1314–1347	... and then to Louis of Bavaria, Germanic king and emperor.
1347–1378	Charles IV of Luxembourg king and emperor.
1348	The Great Plague.
1350	Death of William of Occam.
1356	The "Golden Bull" proclaims the elective principle and sets out the rules regulating the imperial election.
1361–1362	War of the Hanseatic towns against Denmark.
1376	Formation of the League of Swabian towns.
1386	Battle of Sempach.
1400–1410	The Palatin Count Ruprecht becomes king.
1400–1468	Gutenberg.
1414–1418	Council of Constance.
1415	John Hus burnt to death at the stake.
1419–1436	War of the Hussites.
1431–1449	Council of Bâle.
1437	Death of Emperor Sigismond.
1440–1493	Frederick III of Habsburg emperor.
1453	Constantinople falls to the Turks

1473	Birth of Nicolas Copernicus.
1483	Birth of Martin Luther.
1493	Maximilian I crowned Emperor.
1492	Christopher Columbus sails for America.
1517	Luther posts his theses at Wittenberg.
1519	Death of Emperor Maximilian.
1520–1556	Charles the Fifth emperor.
1521	Diet of Worms.
1525	The great Peasant Revolt. Battle of Pavia.
1528	Death of Albrecht Dürer.
1529	Diet of Spires The Turks at the gates of Vienna.
1546	Death of Martin Luther.
1555	Peace of Augsburg.
1576	Death of Emperor Maximilian II.
1576–1612	Rodolph II emperor.
1608	Formation of the Evangelical Union.
1609	Formation of the Catholic League.
1618	Defenestration of Prague. Beginning of the Thirty Years' War.
1619–1637	Ferdinand II emperor.
1620	Battle of the White Mountain. Tilly defeats the Bohemians.
1629	Edict of restitution.
1630	Diet of Ratisbonne—Wallenstein ousted. Gustav-Adolph of Sweden intervenes.
1631	Destruction of Magdeburg by Tilly. Gustav-Adolph continues his advance.
1632	Battle of Rein—Death of Tilly. Death of Gustav-Adolph at Lützen.
1634	Assassination of Wallenstein—Battle of Nördlingen.
1635	France enters the war.
1646	Birth of Leibniz.
1648	Treaties of Westphalia (Münster and Osnabrück).
1681	Occupation of Strasbourg.
1683	The Turks lay siege to Vienna.
1688–1697	War of the League of Augsburg.
1701–1714	War of the Spanish Succession.
1700–1720	Nordic War.
1701	Prussia becomes a kingdom.
1711	Death of Joseph I—Charles VI emperor.
1716	Death of Leibniz.
1717	Belgrade occupied by Prince Eugene.
1729	Birth of Lessing.
1736	Death of Prince Eugene.
1739	Birth of Herder.
1740–1786	Frederick II the Great, king of Prussia.
1740–1780	Reign of Marie-Theresa in Austria.
1740–1742	First war over Silesia.
1741–1748	War of the Austrian Succession.
1744–1745	Second war over Silesia.
1745–1765	Francis I of Lorraine, Germanic emperor.
1749	Birth of Goethe.
1750	Death of Johann Sebastian Bach.
1756	Birth of Mozart.
1756–1763	Seven Years' War.
1759	Birth of Frederick Schiller.
1772	First partition of Poland.
1775	Goethe at Weimar.
1778–1779	War of the Bavarian Succession.
1781	Edict of Tolerance of Joseph II.
1789	French Revolution.
1792	War between revolutionary France and Austria. Battle of Valmy.
1801	Peace of Lunéville.
1804	Napoleon I, Emperor of the French. Francis II resigns the imperial Germanic crown and becomes Francis I, Emperor of Austria.
1805	Austria is defeated by Napoleon.
1806	Confederation of the Rhine—End of the "Holy Roman Empire of Germanic nations".—Collapse of Prussia.
1809	War with Austria.
1813–1815	War of liberation of Europe.
1815	Congress of Vienna—Holy Alliance.
1816	Constitution of Saxony—Weimar.
1818	Constitution of Bavaria.
1819	Conference of Carlsbad.
1827	Death of Ludwig van Beethoven.
1832	Death of Goethe.
1833	Zollverein (Customs union of the Germanic Confederation).
1835	First German railroad.
1848	Revolution
1848–1916	Franz-Joseph emperor
1864	War of Schleswig-Holstein.
1866	War between Prussia and Austria.
1867	Luxembourg is declared neutral
1869	Creation of the Social-Democrat Labor Party.
1870–1871	Franco-German War.

1871 Restoration of the Empire. William I emperor.

1872 *Kulturkampf* in Prussia.

1874 Socialist Party banned in Germany.

1881 Triple Alliance: Germany, Austria, Italy.

1884 First German colonies.

1887 Germano-Russian security treaty.

1888 Year of the three emperors—William II emperor (–1918).

1889 Law on sickness and old age insurance.

1890 Resignation of Bismarck (died in 1898).

1900 Waldersee's expedition in China. First Zeppelin.

1914–1918 First World War—Revolution in Germany.

1919 Signing of the Treaty of Versailles—Ebert president of the Reich.

1920 Entry into force of the Treaty of Versailles—Reparations commissions—French occupation of the Rhineland—Dissolution of the German right-wing private armies.

1921–1922 Unrest, political killings, uprising in Poland, prohibition of the annexation of Austria, negotiations on reparations—Rathenau is foreign minister— signing of the Treaty of Rapallo with Russia.

1923 Occupation of the Ruhr, passive resistance, inflation, Hitler's abortive putsch in Munich, stabilisation of the Reichsmark.

1924 End of the domination of the separatists, elections to the Reichstag, the Dawes Plan, Hitler is pardoned.

1925 Marshal Hindenburg is made President of the Reich (–1934). Treaty of Locarno (Stresemann and Briand).

1926–1930 Unrest, crises, the Young Plan, payment of reparations, polarisation between Communists and NSDAP—Stormtroopers.

1931 World economic crisis. Bank failures. Unemployment.

1932 Rise of Nazism. (NSDAP)—Hitler's candidacy for the Presidence of the Reich—Emergency decrees—Resignation of Brüning—The NSDAP becomes the strongest party—6.6 million out of work—Cabinet under Von Papen.

1933 "Legal" seizure of power by Hitler—Banning of political parties—Law of full powers—Beginning of the dictatorship and the persecution of the Jews, of opponents of the régime and of religious groups. Germany leaves the League of Nations.

1934 Röhmputsch—"Legalisation" of assassination—Death of Hindenburg—Rearmament.

1935 Occupation of the Rhineland—Anglo-German naval agreement.

1936 Berlin Olympic Games—Restoration of compulsory military service—rearmament.

1937–1939 Annexation of Austria and the Sudetenland, reannexation of Memel—1939, annexation of the rest of Czechoslovakia—Hitler-Stalin Pact—Beginning of the Second World War, sought by Hitler.

1939–1945 Second World War—Destruction and surrender of the Third Reich.

1945–1949 Occupation of the four zones by the Allies—Monetary reforms.

1949 Foundation of the Federal Republic of Germany, consisting of the *Länder* of Western Germany.
Konrad Adenauer becomes its first Chancellor.
Foundation of the German Democratic Republic in the Soviet occupation zone.

1955 End of the status of the occupation—the German Democratic Republic joins the Warsaw Pact.

1955 Restoration of an army *(Bundeswehr)* and membership of the Federal Republic of Germany in NATO.

1954–1958 The Federal Republic of Germany joins the Western European Union.
. . . and the European Economic Community (Common Market).

1963–1966 Erhard Government.

1966–1969 Kiesinger Chancellor of the grand coalition.

1969–1976 Governments formed by the SPD and then the FDP, with Chancellors Willy Brandt and his successor Helmut Schmidt.